Transforming Love & Beyond

By

Rayola Kelley

Hidden Manna Publications

Transforming Love & Beyond

ISBN: 978-0-9864066-8-3

Cover Design: Pam Wester

Printed in the USA

Except where otherwise indicated, all Scripture quotations in this book are taken from the King James Version of the Bible.

Hidden Manna Publications
PO Box 3572
Oldtown, ID 83822

Facebook:
https://www.facebook.com/HiddenMannaPublications/

Acknowledgement:

There are a couple of people that have helped me gain some valuable insight into the story I am about to share on these pages. Both of these people are home in glory, but their priceless insight about the culture of the time that is highlighted in this book will begin to make sense to those who approach matters from a western viewpoint. Watchman Nee identified the different stages of love and brought an eastern perspective to the information through his book, "Song of Songs," while the late Ruth Specter Lascelle brought understanding about Jewish practices through her books and personal times of sharing with me.

I also want to thank those who helped to edit this book: my good friend Wanda Heibert and my co-laborer in the Gospel for the last three decades, Jeannette Haley. I also want to acknowledge the valuable work of Pam Wester for her vision and work in doing the covers of our books, including this one. Thank you for making your talent available to us.

Contents

Introduction

This book is a labor of love. It is the second book among the 55 books I have written that fits this unique category. The first book I wrote was my choice, but this one came about because of a suggestion. I wrestled with whether I could do it or not because the story is so incredible, but the suggestion resonated in my spirit in such a way I could not let go of it. I realized at that moment the story had indeed captured my imagination, while stirring my soul and inspiring my spirit.

As I was writing it, I struggled with what to call it. I kept asking myself what word or phrase captures the essence of the story until I realized there are no limitations to the subject matter pertaining to this book. As the title of the book implies, it is about love, but there are different stages to love, and one of the last stages is transforming love. Love must evolve, but real, lasting love is eternal; therefore, each stage of love is a step towards discovering greater aspects of it, and even when you step into the latter stages, genuine love will take you beyond any emotional border and all worldly presentations to catch glimpses of its eternal essence.

During my struggle to do justice to the story, I landed upon a very important question that summarized the journey of love, "What is thy beloved more than another?" This question lies at the core of why we choose to love the people we love. It is hard at times to tell what distinguishes our love. Is it our devotion or feeling of love that magnifies the person, or does that person stand distinct among all others in our hearts, thereby, defining the love that we develop towards him or her, or is it a combination of both?

This story answers the question. As you have gathered, it is love story, but not just any love story. It was written before the foundation of the world, hidden away in types, shadows, and examples. The uniqueness of this story is that it reveals the journey one must often take to discover the beauty and power of sustaining and lasting love that reaches through time, cultures, and hearts to transform the soul.

This book may prove to be a feeble attempt to some to describe a love that often escapes being captured by words, regardless of the nouns, verbs, and adjectives that are used. In some incidents I took some liberty as a means to connect, elaborate or even challenge the reader to consider the inner struggle that might have been going on within the individuals in this book, while striving to maintain the spirit and integrity of the real message.

This book is a simple story of three individuals, which includes myself, who share similarities in their journey to discover the depth, height, and sustaining power of genuine love. Each story will be presented in unison to reveal the similarities as well as the different challenges that each one encountered at the different stages of discovery and growth. The identity of the first two will be obvious while the third companion will be somewhat shrouded in mystery until it is time for her to be unveiled. My goal in presenting the story in this format is to hopefully cause the story to take on greater meaning and life as its message catches the imagination of the reader to actually take flight on the currents of possibilities and promises that are attached to the reality of God's incredible love.

The

Challenge

Throwing Down
the Gauntlet

Sleep is presently escaping me. I sit in my office looking at the blank screen on my computer that is staring back at me. The cursor blinks at me, challenging and taunting me to write something constructive on the page. As a writer who has a possible story dancing around the outer edges of the imagination, there is nothing that seems lonelier and more mocking than a blank screen or piece of paper. Authors will admit the two main challenges in writing a book are how to start it and how to finish it.

I feel many things right now that will not only let me succumb to sweet rest, but which must somehow be expressed. There is a certain awe and wonderment that has flooded my soul, and I know there is a story ready to bust forth out of the recesses of my mind but my soul must land before I will be able to put it into words.

In order to land, I find myself in the quiet of the night resurrecting a memory from the past that I sometimes revisit. I even have a photo of it. I'm sitting on a log on Whidbey Island, Washington, looking out at the ocean. Although I now live in a beautiful part of Idaho, I have discovered that this memory is still a place I can come to, to take captive the inner emotional upheaval that sometimes is unleashed in my soul by circumstances or challenges. There is nothing as calming to my soul as listening to the waves gently washing over the beach. In the distance I can hear seagulls crying out as I breathe in deeply the distinct smell of the salt water of the Pacific Ocean. I sit quietly as the breeze blows across my face, reminding me that even though motion is all around me, the environment allows room for my spirit to become still as peace settles like a gentle covering over my soul.

I come to this place when I have to collect my thoughts. My thoughts are like the waves, restless but advancing toward a destination. At times

8

the wind causes the waves to become overwhelming resembling emotions that begin to be stirred up by unseen currents of thought as I meditate and consider the challenge before me. In a way, the gauntlet has been thrown down for me to consider taking a very important journey that I never expected to take, but my soul has been stirred and inspired by it and will not let it be. The journey I am about to take is not a new journey into uncharted territory; rather, I am about to take a journey back in time while keeping my eye on the future.

The difference in this journey is that I will be taking it with a couple of companions. Although separated by 3,000 years with one companion, the other is still somewhat struggling to emerge from the shadows to come into her own. Nevertheless, these two companions and I still have much in common. In studying both of their journeys I discovered we walked down similar paths. Admittedly, the first time I encountered the first companion, I was confused about her surroundings and her story, while certain aspects of the other remained veiled in many ways. I thought the first companion's story to be a bit too explicit, perhaps on the risqué side, and even though the introduction to my second companion had attracted and challenged me to venture and explore the life I now live as a believer, she was, for the most part, a bit too mysterious and vague for me to define. But I sensed there was so much more behind the events that would shape both of these companions; therefore, I could not let my initial impressions of either one remain as being so. It was clear that my curiosity had been awakened, but at that period in my life I also realized that it was not time for me to attempt to delve any deeper.

As I look back, I recognized that before I could see and understand the similarities we shared, I had to have my own experiences that would produce wisdom and maturity. It was clear that if one is naïve about a matter that requires maturity, he or she will never understand it in the right way. Obviously, before I could take this journey with these two companions, I had to grow up. I am not saying that I have arrived or that there is no room for improvement or growth for as long as I am in this body I will only see and know in part, but the Apostle Paul was clear, we must cease to see and look at life as a child does (1 Corinthians 13:11).

The story you are about to read is a love story. It is not just any love story for it casts incredible shadows across time that have the ability to explode into living color. In the case of my first companion, who started the initial challenge for me to take this journey, her life was recorded in the first of three books written by a man destined to be king, while for the second companion she was being prepared in the wings to take her rightful place beside her king. In the story of the first companion, many believe the writer wrote this poetic book based on a real woman that he secretly admired, and as a result one could almost say it is a fantasy, a story too good to be true, but it is true in so many ways, a parable that spoke of the culture and practices of that day, but clearly held a mystery that would be illuminated centuries later in the unveiling of my second companion. The incident of my first companion was presented in a poetic song, a song that if presented to the public, would have to be presented like an opera in order to present a beautiful contrast in a story form.

The second companion was clearly promised to a king and since she is not identified by name or location, she will be noted at the beginning of each of her sections as the "The Second Companion." Everything about her origins, purpose, and place was ordained even before she was conceived. Both stories were recorded in the oldest book known to the world, a book that does not lie, a book that is forthright about both of my companions and their stories.

The Influence Of Culture

The Coming of
the Age of Cinderella

In order to start this journey, I must begin with me. It is not that I represent the center of significance; rather, it is a matter of establishing what was in order to have a contrast. We are all products of our family and culture. It is amazing to realize that what influences who we are is based on the time and place in which we grew up. It is true, we are individuals who started out with clean slates, and as a result we find that we have been greatly influenced by our culture as to how we express our individuality.

For example, I am a product of the 60's and 70's. I remember the cold war, President John Kennedy's assassination, the riots over the Vietnam War, and the ever growing disillusionment towards God, family, and country. In one generation, many became lost in a drug culture, resulting in aimless wandering, while others rage against all establishment, and some defy all moral restraints.

However, there is one aspect of society that has remained. It centers around America's obsession with sensationalism and love. It seems that much of the American culture is either caught up with iconic sports, or the subject and pursuit of love which is often based on romance which has been sensationalized by fables, movies, and romance novels. In fact, romance is big business and many are trying to tap into it.

Like most young girls growing up at that time, I read and watched stories being played out in songs, books, TV shows, and movies that influenced and inspired my young heart to wish upon a star, to believe that magic existed, and that fantasy could come true. After all, what little princess in her innocent state would not believe or hope for the time when she comes to full bloom as a "Cinderella" patiently waiting in the wings, to be carried away by her prince charming in shining armor, riding in on a white horse to save her from some unfair fate that was enslaving or exploiting her. In her mind when she was finally saved, she would gracefully dance with him between the pages of fanciful expectation into the future to live happily ever after.

As each hopeful princess outgrows the fantasyland of childhood to face the reality of life in general, the innocent notions of living the life of a princess recede into the recesses of the mind to be shut away with childhood memories. Marked as being nothing more than fantasy, the hopes of prince charming give way to puppy love that can prove to be bittersweet, eventually graduating into first love that carries romantic notions that often turn into an emotional rollercoaster ride with great highs and lows as each different and new challenge in any relationship with the opposite sex brings with it. Through it all the princess struggles to come to womanhood, ever wading through romantic presentations propagated by books and movies, and when she finally lands on the runway of reality, romance fizzles out as her prince charming turns out to be some normal guy who neither has a white horse nor is wearing shining armor.

The kingdom that she is often ushered into has no castles, no servants to wait upon her, nor much pomp and circumstance. The music in her mind and dancing in her heart gives way to normalcy and the drudgery of life, as she begins to realize that her husband can prove at times to be the beast, and she could easily "ride on a broom" when life becomes too overwhelming and there appears to be no resolutions for the various irritations and challenges it brings.

As she considers that she is to grow old with this man who no longer excites her as before, she wonders if she can maintain the same level of delight about their relationship in every day drudgery, while enduring the rat race of the times to secure and maintain some type of semblance of life.

I have to admit I understand the above situation, but like the lady in childhood stories, I did meet a real King who proved to be more than my Prince Charming. Clearly, Prince Charming is the image that has been etched out on paper, but my King was not the perfect image conjured up by some author; rather, He proved to be the perfect man who is King.

Right now, I am getting ahead of the story and I need to somewhat digress in time to another girl who no doubt also struggled to come into her womanhood.

The Coming Age
of Womanhood

On the other side of the world, at another time, lived a young woman who was trying to come into her own. She was born into the Jewish culture and lived in 1014 B.C. during a time of peace and great promise when Israel was clearly flourishing as a kingdom under the strong leadership of King David. However, the guard was about to change. His son was being prepared in the wings to take the reins.

One might wonder what a young woman of her status had to hope for. She was a simple Shulamite, from the city of Shunem which was located within the land allotted to the tribe of Issachar.[1] For the most part her tribe seemed insignificant to that of Judah and Levi, even though they had been clearly identified to a very important virtue: that of wisdom.[2] Royalty marked Judah and the priesthood distinguished the Levitical tribe, but like all descendants of Abraham, her heritage was rich because of the Jewish faith that was recorded on Mount Sinai; her inheritance established by the God of heaven, and her possibilities immense. Judah had David and the Levites had Moses and Aaron, but as a woman she had the likes of Sarah, Tamar, Rahab, Ruth, and Abishag. Sarah was used to bring forth Isaac, the promised son, Tamar ensured the lineage of Judah, Rahab produced the Kinsman Redeemer, Boaz, Ruth became the grandmother of King David, and Abishag a Shulamite like herself, was the most prominent person of her time at Jerusalem because she was tending the aged King David.[3]

Granted, there was always the possibility of catching the eye of a king. To be a wife of a king was honorable and desired, but in reality, it

---

[1] Smith's Bible Dictionary
[2] 1 Chronicle 12:32
[3] Genesis 17:19; 21:2-3; 38:24-30; Ruth 4:17-22; 1 Kings 1:1-4; Matthew 1:1-6

simply meant you would eventually become lost in a harem and the only thing that might set you apart is if you became the mother of a future king.

However, in spite of her present realities, as a handmaiden in her society she had the potential to be part of something great, and as a result she had such hope and possibility that allowed her to dream in ways that eluded young women in other cultures. In fact, Jewish handmaidens had one desire that had been passed down from generation to generation and that was to be the mother of the Promised Messiah.[4]

The promise of the Messiah, the seed of woman was first given to Eve in the Garden of Eden after the fall of man. The darkness of sin and death that came upon the soul of man had been penetrated by the wondrous light of this promise. Women such as Hannah, the mother of the great prophet and last judge of Israel, Samuel, had spoken of it when she declared, "The adversaries of the LORD shall be broken to pieces out of heaven shall he thunder upon them: the LORD shall judge the ends of the earth; and **he shall give strength unto his king, and exalt the horn of his anointed.**"[5] (Emphasis added.)

The only daughter of the judge Jephthah bemoaned her virginity upon the mountains of Israel for two months with her companions after her father had rashly vowed to offer the first thing that came out the door of his house as a burnt offering after his great victory over the Ammonites. To his dismay, his only child, his daughter came out the door to greet him with great enthusiasm. He admitted his vow to her and being honorable, she insisted on him keeping it. There is a debate as to whether she was truly offered as a real sacrifice since Yahweh prohibited such practices or whether it meant that she would remain a virgin, never to have the opportunity to bring forth a child, a son, the Messiah, as she would live in seclusion the rest of her life like a widow

---

[4] The late Ruth Specter Lascelle, a Jewish Christian, teacher, and evangelist who grew up in the Jewish faith under the auspice of her grandfather a Rabbi, shared this tidbit with me about Jewish handmaidens' greatest desire was to be the mother of the Promised Messiah and King. When you ponder Mary's humbled prayer in Luke 1:46-55, you see her making reference to this promise.
[5] Genesis 3:15; 1 Samuel 2:10

to fulfill the vow. [6] In fact, the daughters of Israel went yearly to lament the daughter of Jephthah for four days every year.[7]

It was clear from the examples of those who came before the Shulamite, such as Judah's forgotten widowed daughter-in-law, Tamar, the prostitute Rehab, and the Moabite Ruth that Yahweh was not limited to boundaries, lineages, or standing in society. He could choose and use whosoever He willed, allowing a young handmaiden like herself to dare, to dream, and even pray that such an honor as being the mother of the Promised One could befall her.

And, when it came to love, like most young handmaidens she would ponder it. She was part of a culture where the idea of love was often carried on the currents of poetic expression and mysteriously shrouded in veiled images, hidden in everyday examples, and alluded to by promises that echoed through time on the wings of hope. Clearly, love was not the ultimate goal of her culture; rather, it was the preservation of the people of Israel who were not only the apple of God's eye, but the means by which Yahweh would fulfill His promises to Abraham, Isaac, and Jacob, a means in which all nations would be blessed.[8]

Marriages were often arranged in her culture. As in the case of Samson, the Judge, wives could choose to live under their father's authority to ensure their protection from dishonorable husbands. Clearly in arranged marriages, the commitment to love came first, and if one was fortunate enough, the feeling of love would eventually follow.[9]

There was one thing that was clear to her, and that was in her culture marriage was inevitable to ensure the continuance of the nation of Israel, for a woman to be barren in her culture in such a time as she lived would be an unthinkable disgrace.

---

[6] The Jewish name for "LORD" is "YHWH" without vowels and when the vowels are added it is "Yahweh," while the English name is "Jehovah." Since this is in relationship to the Jewish culture, I took the liberty to use "Yahweh."

[7] Judges 11:34-40

[8] Genesis 12:1-3; Psalm 17:8

[9] Judges 15:1-3

Before the Beginning
of Time
(The Second Companion)

It is hard to describe my second companion. What point do you begin from when there is a story to be told? The natural answer is from the beginning, but in the case of this companion, there is no real set date to her entrance on the scene. There are certain events that marked her presence and influence, but her entrance into history can't be definitely identified. Unlike the Shulamite girl and myself, the third companion of this journey can't really be marked by time.

Her story began in eternity, a dimension that cannot be measured. In eternity, what is will be so, what is so has been and will continue to be, and what will be is already so because it is declared as being what is. Clearly, eternity is confusing to us and in our finite state we cannot begin to comprehend that there is no history or future in eternity and that all matters are the present reality of what has already been determined and stands as being so. It is for this reason that the God of heaven introduced Himself as, "I AM THAT I AM."[10] Wherever the Lord is, the past comes together with the present while the future is alive and well, but is simply hidden in the present until it can be unveiled.

There is no distinction in the eternal dimension that is not measured by time, except that which has been marked by some event that simply fulfills what has been declared as being so. God must step into time to bring forth what has already been established in eternity as being true. In the Bible this type of fulfillment of such an event is referred to as, "when the fulness of time was come."[11]

"The fulness of time" simply means that the events happening on earth set forth the right environment for God to bring forth a promise. Romans 11:25 talks about the fullness of the Gentiles and Ephesians 1:10 states, "That in the dispensation of the fulness of times he might

---

[10] Exodus 3:14; Ephesians 1:4,5
[11] Galatians 4:4

gather together in one all things in Christ, both which are in heaven, and which are on earth; even in him."

The plan that the third companion was a part of had clearly existed in the heart of a father. The father had ordained that his son would have a bride, but he was also aware it was not going to be an easy task to secure such a bride. Like Abraham, this father would send a representative to secure a bride among his son's own brethren. Due to his son's standing in the kingdom, it could not be just any bride. It became clear to everyone that the father was willing to pay a high cost as a means to secure a kingdom and a bride for his son.[12]

This is why the story of the third companion is so precious. Even though she had no idea that she had such a call on her life, she would be prepared in an unusual way so that like Queen Esther, she would be ready to meet her bridegroom when the fulness of time was brought forth for her to take her rightful place at her beloved king's side.[13]

This companion's call was determined before her conception and her destiny already established according to an eternal plan. She would find her roots in one particular culture, but her lineage would emerge out of the whole of humanity. Like any bride being prepared, she would be hidden in shadows and chambers until it was her time to be revealed. Her call to this union would be marked by one event that would stand between the history of what was and the history that would become.

Her main purpose would be that of preparation. It was clear she had to be ready for the time her bridegroom called her. According to the culture, their marriage would be agreed upon but the son had to prepare a place for his bride before it could be consummated. In reality, she did not have the freedom to be anything other than what she was ordained to be. It is true she could have resisted the overtures directed at her, but she realized there was no need to resist because everything she ever desired and hoped for was being offered to her. There would be no debate as to her purpose, no culture to define her, no race to distinguish her, and no distinction other than she was chosen.[14]

---

[12] Genesis 24
[13] Esther 2:3, 8, 9; Revelation 19:7
[14] John 14:1-3; 15:16

It was because she was chosen that love was being bestowed on her. She would be adorned with grace, clothed with meekness, and wrapped in incredible promises. However, the preparation would prove to be overwhelming to her at times. She had to remember her initial beginnings. Such memories kept her humble and caused her to remember her dark beginnings that she experienced long before she discovered she had ever been chosen.[15]

---

[15] 2 Peter 1:8,9; Revelation 19:8

The Crisis

The Dilemma

Children are allowed a bit of fantasy to tantalize their imagination and to write across their minds the story of their "happy ever after ending," allowing them to dream that somewhere in a big world there is a place, a garden, and a future event that will usher them into a palace to reign over a benevolent kingdom. However, there is a point where innocence flees, leaving a bewildered adolescent to discover there is a dark side to life. Childish optimism wanes as it becomes evident that things don't always turn out right and that outside of the pages of stories, there are too few princes to go around, and those who exist are clearly on a different plain, running around with a different crowd.

My innocence fled when I was nine. I had to face some not-so-pleasant realities that included my parents divorcing and my brother and I attending an elementary school where elitism was established based on financial status, indifference took on the face of snobbish cliques, prejudice was wielded with a sneering mockery that was expressed with mean, cruel names, and lonely isolation that clearly marked you as you stood friendless on the school grounds. I would try to escape the darkness of my life by reverting to a fantasy world, only to have to come face to face with the challenges plaguing my existence. As the storms raged in my soul, certain rays of light began to penetrate the darkness of my soul and warm my fearful heart. It happened when one particular man entered my life during that great darkness, and amazingly he proved to be my knight in shining armor.

This knight did not ride in on a horse; rather, he walked into my life on crutches. He was not royalty but a sawmill worker who was in an accident where he had badly broken his leg, and as a result he was living on Workman's Compensation. Instead of living in a castle at some imaginary location, he lived in a small mountain community in a small two-bedroom house that was marked with some very interesting holes in the bedroom floor. On my behalf, I witnessed him fearlessly taking on a few dragons and humbling roaring beasts, but not with a sword but with conviction and words. He would also become the husband of another woman, my mother, but my stepfather became my personal knight who introduced a frightened, uncertain young girl to a larger world that included adventurous stories that stirred my troubled imagination into once again dreaming. He exposed me to beautiful classical music that allowed my chaotic emotions to land on the air strip of stability. He enlarged my world with history, politics, and opened a door to possibilities that left me with the ability to consider that I could leave behind more than a simple indentation that would be quickly filled in by those who followed me.

During my teenage years, my life leveled off due to the stability of my stepfather's presence and influence in my life. I lived a typical teenage life, while finding certain freedom in my small school to exceed in certain arenas. I sensed I had a destiny, but I had no clue as to what it was. I thought myself to be wise because I avoided some pitfalls and I saw myself clever because I thought I understood how to get along with others. However, when I left my small world to join the Navy and see the world, I discovered that the world was a bigger version of the elite elementary school I had attended when I was a 4th grader. Granted, I made friends and had new experiences in the military, but I also was aware of loneliness. I was struggling with the issues of life along with a tormenting vacuum I felt in my soul. My soul was clearly empty and the things of the world didn't fill it, the relationships I had couldn't silence it, and the experiences I had seemed to cause a greater void.

I realized everything about ME was in doubt. Clearly, I was in some type of crisis. I had unknowingly been defined by others and even though I cleverly thought that I had figured out how to play the game to get by, I discovered I did not know who I was. I had simply learned to react to my environment, and that such reactions did not stipulate true wisdom or virtue.

It was clear I was in an identity crisis. The person I thought I was, was an illusion and the person I had hoped to be had fallen into some dark abyss. The truth is I had nowhere to turn in order to get my bearings and find out who I really was. I was between a rock and hard place, weary with the endless dead ends that I was mentally encountering.

Granted, there were those who tried to rush in to save the day, and it would have been easy for me to simply let them step in and try to make my life better, but they represented the very things that had set me up in the first place, the very things I was trying to escape. The truth is I wanted to grow up and those who rushed in to save me would have greatly stifled any growth. I couldn't allow such a hindrance. If I survived my experience, I survived; and if I didn't, I didn't, but I couldn't go backwards. I had to keep putting one foot at a time ahead of the other in spite of the fact the path before me was hidden in utter darkness.

There is something about a good crisis that will bring you to a very important place where you are actually forced to face the stark reality of a matter. My challenges in life have taught me to not waste a good crisis; rather, I needed to learn from it, and I must say it is sad to see in the culture of this present day that crises are wasted on young people who hide from maturity in little corners while demanding some pacifier to suck on that will make them feel good about their ineptness and unwillingness to simply face life and grow up in order to grow into who they can be.

It was a crisis that brought ME to a crossroad that would forever change my life. I realized that the darkness I was sensing all around ME, was the darkness of my own soul. I thought myself to be a "good" girl when in reality I had to face that there was a terrible blackness in ME. I thought I had wisdom when in reality I simply had a high opinion of who I thought I was. I saw myself as having decency, but when tested there was no real character behind it.

I didn't really have a name for my darkness, but I knew it was real and I knew it infiltrated every aspect of ME. Those who offered to help ME had no real solution for the darkness that was consuming my inner being. I was groping for something that I was not sure I would recognize or know if I happened to even bump into it. If my inward battle wasn't weighing me down at night with a formidable sense of hopelessness and fear, it was causing the muscles in my body to jump and my nerves to feel like rubber bands that were frayed from being stretched to maximum capacity. There were times I even felt my bed going up and down and I would turn the light on to look underneath, only to find nothing.

I am sure there are those who read this that will draw conclusions as to my plight. Some would say my electrolytes were off. It's true I didn't

24

drink enough water in those days. There might be some that would say that some of it was demonic, which I would tend to agree with, but to what extent would be hard to know. I was void of understanding the spiritual realm even though I was being affected by it.

A light began to penetrate the black darkness of my soul. It started with a book, *The Hiding Place,* by Corrie Ten Boom, which began to illuminate the solution, while hope began to emerge. Grey shadows began to part the darkness as I read tracts about God. Finally, a dental assistant began to part the shadows as he enthusiastically spoke of the man named Jesus Christ while cleaning my teeth.

The light came on when I heard the story of an evangelistic team traveling to an amoral country to share the message of the light, Jesus Christ. They knew the opposition was planning to visibly oppose them in an immoral way, but the Lord kept the time of the meeting from the opposition and it went off without a hitch. I knew that the intervention in that situation was supernatural and I felt something stir within me. However, that was not the end of the evangelistic team's story. They attended an evening service where the pastor explained that those who do not know Jesus Christ were in darkness.[1] When the pastor said the word "darkness" the lights went out in the church. The people, thinking it was a ploy, looked out the windows to see that all the lights were off in the city as well.

The people lit candles and the pastor continued his sermon. As he was wrapping the sermon up, he declared that if they knew Jesus, they could be assured of being children of the light, and in that instant the lights came on.[2]

That simple story took root in my heart. I knew I was in spiritual darkness because I did not know Jesus. Granted, I had heard of Jesus and had sentimental notions about Him because He was born in some manger, but I did not know Him and I certainly did not understand about the light that was associated with knowing Him.[3]

---

[1] Ephesians 5:8; Philippians 2:15; 1Thessalonians 5:2-6
[2] Matthew 4:14-16; John 1:7-9
[3] John 1:4, 5, 9; 8:12

I was faced with a dilemma. I realized that Jesus was the answer to my problem, but if you don't understand what the problem is, you can't properly assimilate the answer. Without the proper understanding the problem will remain vague and unsolvable. Clearly, Jesus was the answer but the darkness kept me from seeing the real problem that plagued my soul.

Unprepared

The Shulamite girl looked around at her mother's vineyard. She was the one who had the responsibility to ensure the quality of it. Granted, there had been some conflict about it because her brothers had their own inheritance to establish, but in the end the lot fell on her to take responsibility for this particular vineyard. She understood her brothers' desire to establish their own legacy for she had the same longing as well. She wanted to establish her own inheritance but she couldn't tend to two vineyards without doing disservice to both.

At this particular stage of life, she was struggling with her part in the vineyard. It was understood by the Jews that the vineyard was Israel and the mother was the great city of Jerusalem. It was up to each Jew to make the necessary investment to ensure the fruitfulness of Israel and the integrity of the spiritual center of Israel, Jerusalem. Yahweh had chosen the Jewish people to fulfill, not only an earthly destiny as a nation, but a spiritual one, and Jerusalem was the chosen city where His very name would be established, stipulating that Jerusalem was to serve as the spiritual center to all Jewish religious activities.[4]

It was clear that her brothers were to establish the physical inheritance of the land, but she was responsible for the spiritual aspect of the legacy. If the unseen inheritance was not maintained, the physical legacy could be lost and would have no real meaning. She had been greatly exposed to worldly activities around her and she was now keenly aware that some of her inner character had been darkened by it, and

---

[4] Deuteronomy 7:6-8; 12:5,6, 11; Song of Solomon 1:6; Nehemiah 11:1,2; Galatians 4:26

that her personal fruit was far from maturity. It was clear as she struggled with her part in the vineyard of Israel that the vineyard of her personal life was lacking.[5] Her affections were undisciplined, her focus was still too self-centered, and her devotion flighty and untrustworthy.

She occasionally thought about how the first man was made from the dust of the earth, somewhat identifying him to the toil that would mark his life and years, but the uncleanness that plagued mankind was not because of the sweat and toil of working in the clay dirt of the earth, but because of the darkness of sin upon his soul. Obviously, man's feet easily became dirty by walking through the world, but what made a man unclean was his deceitful heart and wicked imaginations.[6]

The first man, Adam had been called to dress and keep the garden.[7] As a young girl she often pondered what Adam had to dress or nurture in the garden and what he had to keep or protect in a paradise that was void of weeds and thorns, and stood in perfection as to its fruit and abundance.

As she understood the meaning of these two words, she realized that Adam's real responsibility was to nurture his relationship with his Creator by keeping the environment of the garden free of anything that would disrupt his fellowship with Yahweh.[8] He had been entrusted with dominion over creation so that he could serve as protector over it in order to guard the life he had with his Creator. However, when he allowed the serpent in, Adam failed to oversee and protect the wellbeing of the garden. The serpent waited in the wings for the right time to entice Eve with lies that set her up to fall into transgression, and Adam standing near her and witnessing the temptation, willingly took of the deadly fruit that would put all of his descendants under a death sentence. She understood she had an inherent disposition that caused a separation from her Creator, but Yahweh gave the Law on Mount Sinai that

---

[5] Song of Solomon 1:5, 6
[6] Genesis 3:17-19; Jeremiah 17:9,10; Matthew 15:10-20; John 13:5-11; Romans 3:23; 5:12-14
[7] Genesis 2:15
[8] Taken from Strong's Exhaustive Concordance of the Bible. "Dress" points to bond-service that serves as a form of worship (5647), while "keep" means to guard, hedge about, mark, preserve, observe—save self (8104).

stipulated that the blood of acceptable offerings could cover the people's sins, allowing them to approach Him on the basis of covenant that He had made with Abraham, Isaac, and Jacob.[9]

In her inner struggle to come to terms with her place in the vineyard she was aware that every Jew had a great calling and purpose, but it could only be realized on a personal basis. Perhaps her spiritual problem was that there was no grand place to focus her attention on. Granted, there was the tabernacle, a mere tent that housed the prized furnishings of the ark, the candlestick, and the altars but it did not seem sufficient enough to truly bear or represent Yahweh's name, Creator and Maker of all. King David wanted to build the temple but the prophet, Nathan, informed him that since he was a man of war, the building of the temple would fall to his son, Solomon, who would prove to be a man of peace.[10]

Solomon was not yet king and the prospects of a temple being built was yet to happen but she could somewhat console herself that there would be a temple and it would speak of the greatness of Yahweh. Meanwhile, she was aware of the great call upon her people to serve as the light in the midst of idolatrous paganism. Since she was Jewish and beginning to work in the vineyard, she was becoming more and more aware that she was part of that calling.

As she struggled with her spiritual condition, she realized that her spiritual well-being had nothing to do with a physical temple but her own relationship with Yahweh. She had to consider if she was truly prepared to take her place in her personal vineyard. She knew that her spiritual inheritance was hers to claim, but to lay claim to it she sensed she would expose her own spiritual ineptness that would leave her feeling vulnerable and undone.

---

[9] Genesis 1:26; 3:6; Ephesians 4:14; 1 Timothy 2:14; Hebrew 9:22
[10] Exodus 19:5,6; Deuteronomy 14:2; 2 Samuel 7:1-16; 1 King 5:2-5; 6 (Solomon's name means "peaceful.") Meaning of name taken from Smiths' Bible Dictionary.

The Auction Block
(The Second Companion)

Born in slavery, the struggling girl looked into the bleak future seeing no way out of her plight.[11] She had dreams but in her present state it was futile for her to hang on to any hope of seeing them coming to fruition. There was no expectation of a purposeful life, no confidence of deliverance from her present state, and no future to call her own.

She realistically knew her fate. She had been put on the auction block for the highest bidder to purchase. She was examined, judged, touched, prodded, and mocked. To many she was a mere specimen, a piece of property at best and a mere asset that could be once again sold down the line if the master was not pleased.

Her present master was harsh, cruel, and abusive. He had not started out that way. At first, he had given her the impression that he would bestow everything on her she could imagine if she would consent and play along with him.[12] She failed to realize it was nothing more than a sick game.

He had promised her a palace in which she could be queen, but instead she became a substandard servant who would serve at his tables but never enjoy the abundance of them. He promised her happiness, but she lived in misery. He pointed to the immense wealth of his kingdoms, but she was now living in utter poverty. Her master's presentation of the life she would live and experience was a façade, an utter lie.[13]

She was not only a slave, but she was now captive to an environment that robbed her of any hope of life, ensnared her affections in an endless maze of disillusionment, and had caused a blanket of depression to enfold her soul. The darkness that was consuming her was so stifling, she felt at times her breath escaping her, leaving her in a state of panic. Some spoke of the dawning of a new light, but in her

[11] Romans 5:12, 14; 6:20,21; 7:14-17
[12] Luke 4:5,6
[13] Matthew 4:14-16; John 8:44; 10:10; John 16:11; 2 Corinthians 4:3,4

estimation the light would never be able to penetrate the great darkness that held claims to her soul.[14]

In the mind of the slave, she had nowhere to turn. She could not buy, earn, or secure her freedom from her master. She was clearly at the mercy of one who proved to be cruel and taunting towards her. It was becoming clear that she was hopelessly indebted to a masochist who demanded sick pleasures, but never offered true delight to those who serve at his bidding.

In the past she had cried out into empty space beseeching what she hoped to be a merciful God. Her cries became more prevalent when she felt tormenting desperation take hold of her soul as she became more aware that she was becoming old before her time due to the filth of her slavery which encrusted her into a state of despair. But, she felt that her cries were swallowed up by the vast nothingness that lay before her.[15] If only she could dare to dream that there was some master who would see her plight, recognize her potential, and be willing to sell all he had to purchase her with the intent of making her a bride, a princess, maybe not of a great kingdom, but of his heart and household.

As she thought about the "if only," these two words once again floated into the vacuum of the crowded marketplace, becoming an echo that only her soul could hear as they became lost in the darkness of her personal despair.

It was clear that she was now spent out and useless to her master. To prove it to the world, she was on the auction block to be sold off for whatever price her master could manage to receive for a servant, who in his mind, no longer had redeemable qualities that would mark her as a prized possession. In her mind, she had to agree with him, and perceived that no one would desire her in her present state. She was washed up in many different ways and was resolved to accept her hopeless fate because she had no other choice.[16] She felt like an old faithful horse ready to be put out to pasture by the owner, but she feared

---

[14] Romans 3:10, 23; James 1:13-15
[15] Proverbs 13:15
[16] Psalm 103:15,16; 1 Peter 1:24

if her new owner was like the last one, there would be no mercy, but rather a terrible end for her.

She suddenly sensed something penetrating her soul. She looked into the crowd to see if what she sensed was her imagination. It was as if time stopped still and the people parted as her eyes quickly landed on a man who was standing quietly before her. She was being drawn to him in a way she could not explain. She felt undone by his look, but at the same time hope was rising out of a deep pit. He did not wear kingly robes, yet she perceived he was royalty. Unlike the rest who sized her up as a piece of property, he was seeing her as a person.

His eyes were full of love and compassion, and even though he was looking at her, she could not imagine that such virtues were actually directed at her even though he was not looking past her, through her, above her, or around her; rather, he was looking at her. She couldn't imagine what he was seeing in her, a slave from birth, used up by her ruthless master, spent out for the pleasures of others, void of strength, and stripped of all beauty, but yet, she sensed he saw some type of hidden beauty and potential in her.

The bidding began. Her master had offered the first bid in order to get the bidding started. Even though he considered her past her prime, he was not about to let her go cheaply. After all, he wanted as much as he could get for her. She gasped as the next bid came from the stranger with the loving eyes she felt drawn to.

It was clear from the tone of her master's voice that he felt he had a live one on the hook and he was going to see how far the bidder would go. As the bid went higher and higher, it struck her that her cruel master enjoyed the game that he was now in. At such times, he didn't care how much money the stranger bid, he simply bid higher in order to come out on top of what had suddenly become a competition to him. She knew her master well enough to know that he would figure if he lost the money for her this time around, he could still sell her to someone else, but for some reason he could not lose to this man.[17]

---

[17] Isaiah 14:13,14

As the bidding intensified, her master began to sweat as anger boiled to the surface at the prospect of losing to this foolish man. Out of complete frustration, he yelled, "How much do you plan to bid on her?"

The stranger quietly stared at her master. Then, in a quiet voice, he asked her master a question. "What are you offering for her?"

Her master declared, "I oversee many kingdoms and I can offer them all for her if I choose."[18]

The stranger asked her master, "What is she to you?"

"She is my servant. I own her and her destiny is in my hands," responded her master in his usual arrogant manner.[19]

"What do you require of her as your servant? "the stranger asked.

"I own her and could take her off the auction block any time I choose, and I could require everything she has including her very soul!"

The stranger's eyes narrowed at her master. "The bidding has already begun; therefore, you have relinquished your right as her master until all bidding has been stopped."

Her master drew back as if he had been slapped by some unseen force, but he mustered enough sense to ask the stranger a question. "And, just what do you have to offer for her?"

The stranger answered with quiet authority, "All that is in my father's storehouse."[20]

The girl couldn't believe that this stranger would give all that was in his father's storehouse for her. She couldn't imagine how this man would value her in such a way that he would give all of his inheritance for her, and as she looked at her master, she sensed that he knew this man's father and the riches that were in his father's storehouse. "How do I know that you have the authority to offer all of the treasures of your father's storehouse for her?" her master asked.

"Everyone here knows my relationship with my father including you. All that my father owns is mine. I am his voice, hands, and eyes, but to confirm that my father has given me all authority, I have the necessary

---

[18] Matthew 4:8,9
[19] Romans 6:20,21
[20] Psalm 68:19; Malachi 3:10; Ephesians 1:3-14; Philippians 4:19

document with me, and I can assure you that I have more than enough to surpass your bid."[21] He then handed the auctioneer the document.

The auctioneer's eyes widened as he looked at the legal parchment. He then looked at her master and nodded his head to confirm the man's claims.

The auctioneer looked at the crowd. "It is clear that we are at an impasse. It would not serve either one of these bidders to continue on." He looked at each bidder. "What do you two want to do?"

Her master quickly spoke up. "Are you blind?" he cried out in frustration at the stranger. "Can't you see her state? She has lost all real value even to me as a servant! She stands before you in rags and filth![22] Let me take her now and you can keep your father's storehouse intact. After all, I would hate to see you invest so much in one such as her"

"If she has lost all real value to you, why would you not sell her to me and be done with her?" the stranger asked.

"I don't understand why you would want to buy her!" Her master's anger began to peek around the edges of his frustration. "What will you do with her?"

"I will make her my bride," the man quietly answered.[23]

Her surprised gasp was lost in the astonished response of the crowd who by now was captivated by the exchange that was taking place before the auction block.

The stranger looked around at the crowd. "Let it be known that the document I have handed to the auctioneer verifies that I have already purchased this woman; therefore, she is now free to choose her master."[24]

He looked at her with the same penetrating look of love. "You now must choose whom you will follow, your former master or me."

She couldn't believe her ears. She was free to choose? She had never had the opportunity to choose anything for herself and it seemed so strange. She felt drawn towards her despotic master because of

---

[21] Matthew 28:18; John 14:9-11; Colossians 2:9
[22] Isaiah 64:6; Romans 7:18
[23] Revelation 19:7
[24] Matthew 6:24

familiarity, even though it was sick and nightmarish. Trickles of fear were beginning to rise up at the prospect of following a stranger into the unknown.[25]

Granted, the man had promised everything she had hoped for, but after being lied to so many times by her former master, how could she trust him to do as he said? Besides, the thought of her being his bride in her present state seemed like a mockery, a terrible joke even to her.

As she considered her options, she realized there were not two options but only one right answer. If she chose neither one to be her master and simply walked out into the world, she realized from previous examples, she would be taken captive by one of her master's associates and brought under his auspice once again. It was clear in her mind, there was only one right choice. She would choose to go with the stranger, and just as she made the decision, she felt the chains fall away from her feet and her hands. She was set free from the unseen shackles that had bound them tightly together.[26]

The auctioneer handed her the document. It fell open and she could not believe her eyes. On it were words written in red, "PAID IN FULL."[27]

The stranger walked over to her. She noticed he had a sweet smile on his face, revealing how pleased he was at her decision. His hand reached up to her to help her down from the auction block in order to begin a new journey with her. Clearly, this man had not only captured her attention, but was now taking hold of her heart in a way she could not describe. As her hand touched his, an awakening went through her whole body. It was then that she knew her life would never be the same again.

---

[25] Matthew 16:26
[26] Isaiah 10:27; Luke 4:18,19
[27] Luke 9:56; John 19:30; 1 Timothy 2:6

Initial Love

Drawn By Love

I cannot tell you the exact minute that I realized that I had discovered real love. To me author, Janette Oke best described how I encountered this love in the title of her book. "Love Comes Softly."

At the time it happened I really could not tell you what I was expecting. I knew that my soul was a barren wilderness and it was clear that my life was empty and the things and activities of the world could not fill it. In my pathetic state I felt a gentle drawing towards God to discover the answer to my spiritual vacuum, but I had no idea where to look and what I was looking for.

I had been involved in religion, but it was clearly man-made and man-centered and put a greater burden on me to be something I was not, while failing to answer the nagging questions of my soul. At the time, I couldn't see the hand that was situating circumstances so that I could be in the right place, at the right time, and around the right people who would lead and point me to the right solution. Neither did I realize that love was quietly walking up behind me in preparation to walk beside me.

I was still in the Navy when it happened, stationed at the amphib base in Coronado, California. I had spent two years at Pearl Harbor and had less than a year left when new orders came through that would send me to Norfolk, Virginia. Without knowing it, I rejected the orders by requesting that they let me finish out the rest of my enlistment in Hawaii.

Unbeknown to me, that unseen hand was behind the events. While home on leave during Christmas holiday I was issued new orders to Coronado. My possessions went to the East Coast, while I went to the West Coast, to eventually be reunited a few weeks later.

It was at Coronado that the Lord would bring two women my way. They were cousins, Joan and Mary Ellen Munyon, and I would meet them through my boot camp friend I stayed with for a couple of months until her husband came back from Westpac. My friend served with Joan in the Navy. It was these two cousins who quietly listened to my conceited ramblings about what I thought I knew about God, patiently waited for me to ask the right questions concerning God, made themselves available to take me to the right places where I would hear the truth, and silently suffered with and through my immaturity and flawed character, all the while serving as living examples of true Christianity.

There are five distinct memories that surround these women. The first one was when I met Joan for the first time. She was kind enough to drive me to the base for my daily work because my friend had to stand duty during the early morning. It was on our way to the base that we talked religion. Needless to say, I showed my ignorance and she quietly revealed her wisdom by listening and then responding in a gentle manner.

The second memory I have is the night my roommate had the two cousins over to dinner. We got on the subject of God and faith and it was during that time I had an impression to ask them if they would take me to church with them. They agreed.

The third event happened at church. These two cousins had to travel quite a distance to pick me up for church. When I walked into the sanctuary of the church, I sensed something different and before I left that church, I recognized what it was. I had encountered the glorious presence of the love of God. I couldn't tell you the sermon that was preached that day, but I walked away with a sense of God and I understood that I needed Jesus Christ to turn my upside-down world, right side up.

The fourth event was seeing and hearing Corrie Ten Boom in person. It was her book, *The Hiding Place* that had caused hope to arise in my soul, and as if God was handing me a special gift, she came to San Diego a couple of weeks before my discharge from the Navy. My two patient mentors had heard the news and asked me if I would like to go with them to hear her. Nothing could have kept me from seeing her. She was as inspiring in person as she was in her book. Her book had caused hope to penetrate my great spiritual darkness, but her simple explanation of the Gospel by using the illustration of a flashlight brought greater clarity to me about Jesus saving my soul by taking away my sin.[1]

We do not know how heavy something is until we cease to be under the burden of it. The burden of my sin was great and as the love of God penetrated the darkness of my soul with the hope of Jesus, the great burden began to lose its grip on my soul, and as the understanding of Jesus' redemption took root, the burden took flight.[2]

It's hard to describe what I felt, but it was glorious. I felt cleansed, making me feel young and alive once again and there was a certain giddiness to my walk. My love for Jesus was fresh, my joy bubbling up, and my excitement indescribable. I sensed I was on a new adventure where I would discover wondrous treasures along the way that would enrich my life in ways I could never imagine.[3]

The fifth event turned out to be my first encounter with the Holy Spirit. The cousins had me over for dinner a few days before my discharge. They wanted to send me away with a prayer and their blessings. I will never forget what happened. As they prayed for me, I felt light headed and it was as if I was being lifted off of my feet, while being enfolded by incredible warmth and peace. I had a sense that the Lord was allowing me that moment to put a stake down to remind me that He is more real than the physical world, and that He must be experienced in a personal way to remain real and alive in the heart.

It was on the plane on my way home after my discharge that I realized that a new chapter was beginning in my life. In a way, the Lord was preparing me for the path set before me. As the plane began descending to land at my destination, the sunset was displaying the most beautiful colors. The vibrancy of it was assuring me of a colorful journey, one that would be marked by changes, followed by the twilight of possibilities that would give way to the darkness of testing. Each change would prepare me to stand in assurance that, as in my initial experience, the heavenly light would ultimately part the darkness, once

---

[1] Hebrews 10:4, 9-19
[2] Matthew 11:28-30; John 3:16-18
[3] 2 Corinthians 5:17

38

again bringing clarity and understanding of God's faithful love and commitment towards me.

Unexpected Encounter

The Shulamite girl was totally unprepared. She had faithfully worked in the vineyard, but the world was pulling at her to fling all to chance and pursue her own desires. She would never have suspected that her sense of duty had placed her in the right location at the right time.

The problem with working in the vineyard is that one is not prepared or ready for any unexpected intrusions, but an unexpected intrusion came. The king came to her vineyard. Like all of Israel, she had heard about the king. His name meant "peace" which served as its own healing ointment for a kingdom that was plagued by war, but she never imagined that he would ever grace her life with his presence, let alone give her an unexpected invitation.

Like most young handmaidens, she relished any possibility that the king might look upon her. She had thought about the young vibrant man who was being readied to take the throne of Israel. He was a fine specimen, and like most loyal subjects she had developed an affection for him.[4] Of course, it was just an affection that had no real substance to it because a personal relationship had not been developed, and from her perspective, probably never would be.

Love requires an investment and her imagination allowed the king to simply capture her affections out of a type of loyalty, but then came the day that the king came by way of her vineyard. Needless, to say, she was unprepared to meet him in his kingly robes. She thought of the future king's white linen curtains in his residences, rightfully representing the righteousness his innocence seemed to exhume, but she was like the tents of Kedar that were dark, revealing her inner condition. She was covered from the dirt of the earth, swept up by the demands of the world, that were clearly highlighted with the sweat of her activities. She looked dingy and when the king stood in her midst and looked her way, she felt

---

[4] Song of Solomon 1:2, 3

black and unworthy. When he acknowledged her she felt undone and humbled.[5]

How could a king even consider her in her present state? Young handmaidens were prepared for months ahead of time with special treatment and presented in suitable attire for the king's approval and acceptance. It was this very realization that made her affections take flight to soar in great expectation of the possibilities.[6] She wanted to run to him and perhaps experience his goodness, and possibly his love, but her state prevented her, robbing her of any inclination to seek after him

However, an unexpected desire rose up to take hold of her heart. She realized she no longer was willing to have a casual knowledge of him, she wanted an intimate relationship with him, but until there was some type of invitation, she dared not act upon her desire alone. She knew she had to be drawn, given some indication that she was to seek after him.[7]

It was as her desire took flight that suddenly she felt that drawing. She wouldn't simply seek after him, she would run after him, and when she caught up to him, she found herself being brought into his chambers.[8]

In his chambers, gladness made her heart throb with unspeakable joy. Clearly, she was not in his chamber because she was special but because of his love. She had heard from others that his love was more intoxicating and satisfying than anyone could imagine and now she was experiencing its wondrous grace for herself. She recognized that he was honorable in his love; therefore, he didn't use it to exploit, use, or abuse those who were vulnerable or those who were seeking for it.

As she rejoiced for being in his chamber, she wrestled with the question, "Why her?" She had not been prepared to stand before him, let alone meet him, and now she was in his chamber. Any mirror would have revealed her state and even though she knew that beauty was possible it was hidden under a layer of dirt and sweat.

---

[5] Song of Solomon 1:5,6
[6] Esther 2:2,3
[7] Song of Solomon 1:4; John 6:44; James 4:8-10
[8] Song of Solomon 1:4

In the light of his chamber she knew that she would be exposed. It was clear that her appearance had already caused conflict, especially within her own soul. There was always much to do amid the activities and demands of the vineyard, leaving little time to prepare her own vineyard to produce pleasing fruits fit for a king.

There was no way she could stand before the king in her present state, but there was no time to change her present status.

Too Good to Be True
(The Second Companion)

What does a king look like? In the girl's world of slavery, her treacherous master was a prince over many kingdoms, making him a type of god over various systems.[9] He entertained, parlayed with, and used various people who held titles and who were in high positions in different arenas of the world to control and manipulate those who were willing to sell their souls to him. They may have worn different styles of clothes and represented different interests, but in the end they each proved to be of the same caliber as her master. For the most part they were selfish, self-centered, and self-serving, and if they took note of her at all, she was not respected as a human being, but merely as an object to be used to promote their own pleasure and self-importance.

These so-called elites may have had earthly possessions, but they proved to be poor in character as they demonstrated that they were void of ethical clarity and honorable conduct.[10] They dressed like kings, but in reality, they were nothing but immoral, spiritual paupers.

However, her new master was a king but he was modestly dressed. The slave girl had learned to listen well and she picked up a few bits of information about her new master as they made their way through the throngs of people that were going about their daily routines. He had been destined to be king by his father, but he was born in an uncertain time and in a humble setting that would not be considered acceptable

---

[9] John 12:31; 14:30; 16:11; 2 Corinthians 4:4
[10] Matthew 19:23-26; James 2:5

by anyone, especially royalty. He had clearly been declared and recognized by others as king, but it was obvious by the attitudes of his own people that his kingdom was somewhat mysterious and had not been fully established in a manner that would cause the world to recognize it as being legitimate or important.[11]

She considered life unfair, but the present contrast made her aware that it was not the clothes or the position that made a man; rather, it was his inner character. Men often wear clothes to hide their real character, but those who possess true character are clothed with humility that is not only reflected through their mannerisms, but causes even their clothes to look like royalty. Ironically, the fools ride on the high horse of royalty above the crowds, while real royalty walks among, and with, the common people.[12]

Her new master graciously placed the coat he had been wearing around her to hide the filth of her appearance.[13] Her attire was in rags, her skin was caked with the filth of the streets, her arms and legs marked by the chains of the auction block, and her countenance weighed down by the utter despair of her slavery.

She could smell his fragrance on his coat. How sweet it was to her nose, but she was keenly aware that underneath it was the foul smell of her state.[14] It was the smell of things that had gone sour and were now being consumed by rot and decay in a cold tomb of indifference.

She could not imagine what it would feel like to be clean.[15] She had felt so dirty for such a long time that she couldn't fathom experiencing that which was pure, soft, and desirable.

As she was being escorted to her new abode, she pondered whether her new master was telling the truth. She felt unworthy to be his slave, but the idea that he was taking her home to make her his bride made her feel even more undone and unworthy. Greater despair gripped her soul as she realized there was no way she was ready to be a bride,

---

[11] Matthew 2:1-6, 10-11; Luke 1:31-33; John 1:11; 18:36
[12] Ecclesiastes 10:6,7; 1 Peter 5:5
[13] Luke 15:22; 1 Corinthians 1:30
[14] 2 Corinthians 2:15,16
[15] Isaiah 64:6

presented to such a benevolent king, and in her mind, she silently questioned if she ever would be.

She knew his servants would try to take the smell and filth of the pigpen of the world off of her, but could they take the wretched ways of the pigpen out of her? They might prepare her body as best as they could, but how would they change her barren soul as to how she saw herself and felt about her potential?[16]

In light of the endless indictments that were coming at her, she felt hopeless. Surely, as soon as she stood in the full light, he would see her condition and rethink his decision to make her his bride. It was clear to her that she had nothing to offer him and if anything was accomplished, it would be because of him continually looking beyond her present state, and seeing her unknown potential.

She wrestled with the ironic reality that what was happening to her was surreal, surely a dream that would eventually prove to be too good to be true.

Facing Obstacles

I began my spiritual journey flying high on expectations that were based on assumed religious notions. I had an incredible salvation experience when I first encountered the Lord's love, and I was lifted up on wings of joy by His presence as I realize that what had plagued my soul, my past sins, had been dealt with. But I did not realize that much of my excitement was an immature zeal that lacked real knowledge about the character of God.[17]

My love for my new Lord and Savior was fresh and vibrant. His cross stood before me, casting an indelible line in time.[18] On one side were those in utter, complete darkness and on the other side was the glorious light of His love and salvation. I knew how great the darkness was on the one side, but because of experiencing His love, confessing my sin, and receiving His life, I stood on the side of His light, reveling in my

---

[16] Hebrews 10:22
[17] Romans 10:2, 3
[18] John 3:16-21

salvation. After all, I now had a token of His love—the cross and the knowledge of His life taking root in my soul.

Initial love has a certain excitement to it but it must be tested to grow, often causing abrupt landings to take place on the airstrip of reality. Such excitement will quickly wear off when drudgery and challenges begin to insert themselves into every day existence. Hindsight eventually revealed to me that the Lord had initially given me a taste of heaven to serve as a point of remembrance to stand against the day when obstacles began to mount, and mount they did.

The Lord had initially called me to come and walk beside Him, but now I had to follow Him along an uncertain path. I thought I understood what was required of me, but it came from a sense of religious duty of being pious, which required me to practice some moral restraints and walk in good deeds, without realizing I was missing the mark of what was excellent.[19]

At the time I did not understand iniquity. Iniquity are those flaws in your moral character that will cause you to be vulnerable in times of temptation, raw when insulted, and defeated when tested. I had no idea that I had such flaws in me because I considered actions more than character. A person can be decent enough in action, while harboring great moral flaws. We can deceive ourselves about such flaws because we have no intention of giving way to them, but in temptation, it is not intention that is being tested, but character.[20]

We often judge ourselves based on our intentions, but intentions are fickle when the motivation is wrong and sound character hasn't been established to properly discern them. The Bible is clear that the ways of a man are clean in his own eyes, but the Lord weighs our spirits or motivations.[21]

My intention was to do right, but like Paul I found myself falling into traps and ending up doing wrong.[22] I would lecture myself about how I

---

[19] Proverbs 14:12; 16:25; Romans 3:23
[20] James 1:13-15
[21] Proverbs 16:2
[22] Romans 7:14-24

handled a matter, only to be handled by the matter, and miserably failing to overcome the moral flaws that were besetting me in my Christian life.

I was striving hard to read my Bible, attend church, stand for what was right, and live according to some religious code without realizing that such attempts did not win me Brownie points with the Lord. After all, these activities were for my personal edification, and necessary for any real growth to take place, as well as reasonable when it came to service. I would eventually learn they had nothing to do with pleasing God.[23]

I failed to realize my ideas were based on past experiences, and that my life in Christ was to be a new experience.[24] I started off with assumptions only to experience utter defeat in the end. The Lord gave me a lot of rope to veer off into left field to do my own thing while missing what real Christianity was all about.

Relationships grow as love grows, trust develops as the level of commitment is unveiled in times of testing, and fading zeal must be replaced with sobriety that enables one to honestly face a matter.[25] Since I thought I could handle matters and ultimately do right, I found my attempts falling flat, leaving me feeling deflated and defeated, which caused the joy of my salvation to decline.

My initial excitement for the Lord wouldn't allow me to imagine that my love for Him would ever fade, but fade it did. My attitude showed not only my immaturity, but my arrogance, revealing that all such self-sufficiency finds its platform in pride that swings from the heights of silly notions. Such arrogance teeters on pinnacles of fantasy that will cause one to easily slide into disillusionment.[26]

I clearly was teetering on the pinnacle, but I found myself falling off of it to face the reality of my character. I knew Jesus died for my sins, but I thought something was salvageable in me. It took falling off the pinnacle to come face-to-face with my true condition. Jesus' blood took away my sin, but I still had the "old man" calling the shots and a worldly attitude that had not been transformed.[27]

---

[23] Hebrews 11:6
[24] 2 Corinthians 5:17
[25] 1 Peter 5:8-10
[26] Romans 12:3; 1 Corinthians 10:12; 2 Corinthians 3:5; Galatians 6:3
[27] Romans 12:1,2

I didn't realize that there was nothing good in me that God could accept; therefore, whatever found its source in the "old me" was not acceptable to God. I failed to see that I made my relationship with the Lord about "religious doing" instead of developing a mature relationship with Him.

The Lord had called me, but now He needed to separate me from my immature notions to Himself. I had my own ideas of what the Christian life meant, as well as the influences of others who had their own array of religious ideas and notions, but none of it was in line with God's desire for me to discover my identity and life in Him.

I knew something was terribly wrong in my spiritual life, but each time I tried to figured it out, I came out at the same empty place that was marked by failure. Eventually, I was brought to the place where I had to face my wretched state and what I was missing. I was missing the reality of Jesus. In my religious pursuits, I had missed coming to the knowledge of Him.[28]

The reality of my foolishness broke me into many pieces. I had clearly failed to hit the mark of my calling and purpose in Christ, and even though the Bible had been clear that there was no good thing in the flesh and that the best that comes from the flesh is considered to be as filthy rags before God, the truth of it was drowned out by my "religious" activities. It became clear from the depths of my despair that outside of knowing and possessing Christ there was nothing salvageable in me. I was undone by the revelation of His goodness and felt unclean by the iniquity that had often raised its ugly head in different ways to rule my emotions and drive my youthful lusts.[29]

I was overwhelmed by the reality that in my search to know God's Word, I failed to discover and know Him. I had head knowledge about His Word, but there was no heart revelation of Him. As I laid in complete brokenness, I realized I had left my initial love for Jesus behind to pursue knowledge of Him, and failed to discover Him. The result was the Written Word had become dead-letter because the Living Word was missing.[30]

---

[28] Proverbs 3:5-7; Jeremiah 29:13; Philippian 3:8,10
[29] Isaiah 64:6; Romans 7:18; 2 Timothy 2:22
[30] Romans 7:6; 1 Corinthians 8:1-3; 2 Corinthians 3:5,6; Revelation 2:4

The whole fiasco made me realize that my world was in ruin, the joy of my salvation was gone, and my religious activities had become a bitter pill to my soul. As I began to cry out to God in brokenness, confession, and helplessness, the Lord graciously met me in love, mercy, forgiveness, and grace.

I had an incredible sense of His mercy consuming my grief as His grace flowed downward and His Spirit enfolded me in His forgiveness. I felt clean and revived. I knew I was underserving of His lovingkindness, but with a renewed joy I received His forgiveness and cleansing with gladness. I remember jumping up from my prostrate position on the floor with so much excitement that I wanted to tell the whole world that Jesus was real, but I felt His hand of restraint upon me. His instruction that followed was simple, "First, learn of Me."[31]

We cannot know who we are in Christ until we learn who Christ is. We need to first learn where and how to feed on that which is truly nourishing to actually discover what we have in Christ and come to a place of real satisfaction and rest in Him.

I'll never forget the next invitation that came from Him in preparation for learning of Him. He invited me to His banqueting table. There was even an empty chair waiting for me to come, sit down, and truly learn what it would mean for me to partake of Him.

The Right Mirror

The inner struggle was real for the Shulamite handmaiden. How could she stand in the light of the king's chambers without her appearance being fully exposed?[32] She shuddered to think of how the king would view her without the proper preparation. Surely, he would regret his invitation to her once the light revealed the extent of the world's defilement upon her soul, but there was nowhere to hide, no place to run to, and no means to change her appearance.

---

[31] Matthew 11:28, 29
[32] Song of Solomon 1:6

It became obvious, as she waited for some type of response from the king, that she recognized that her soul was longing for a more intimate relationship with him. His concern and regard told her that their relationship would be more than just that of a king to a subject, but that of a shepherd in regard to the welfare of the sheep. She became keenly aware that she wanted to be part of his flock, but she had to find where he led his sheep to feed because she knew once they were satisfied, they could rest. It was clear that her toil in the vineyard had caused an anxiousness that kept her from coming to a true place of rest in his presence. She no longer wanted to follow men who had some point of association with the king, but she wanted to follow the King, who had a shepherd's heart, to the true place of spiritual nourishment, satisfaction, and rest.[33]

As she thought about her plight, she was suddenly reminded of how Yahweh had found Israel before Moses led the people to the Promised Land. As a people, they had been enslaved, afflicted, driven by harsh taskmasters, and buried by the toil and sweat of the demands of the world they existed in. It was Yahweh that bore them on eagles' wings and lifted them above their bondage and brought them to Himself in the wilderness to meet them at Mount Sinai.[34]

It struck her that it was not how she saw herself that mattered; rather, it was how the king saw her. She needed to see herself, not from the mirror of the world, but the mirror of his eyes. The handmaiden also would know by his attitude and response towards her how he actually perceived her.

It was the king's words that brought to rest her concerns about her plight. It was as if he read her mind and knew what bothered her as he addressed her as the, "fairest among women."[35] He was identifying her as one being beautiful, goodly to consider, pleasant to be with, and suitable in character.[36]

---

[33] Song of Solomon 1:7
[34] Exodus 19:4
[35] Song of Solomon 1:8
[36] Strong's Exhaustive Concordance of the Bible, (3303)

In her present state, would she dare believe the king's description? Yet, the king was known for his trustworthy character. He was not reputed to be a liar, nor was he one who cons to get his way or flatters to seduce. It was clear that she had to trust his character if she was going to receive his estimation of her. After all, he not only saw her as being beautiful, but that she stood out among others as being distinct to him, one whom he had actually chosen to stand in such a place.

To confirm her distinction, the king entrusted her with the responsibility of going forth to feed those outside his tent of communion who were even more immature than she.[37] He was actually entrusting her with something precious to him. How that spoke volumes to her!

It was then that the king went on to describe her beauty as he saw it. He compared her to a company of horses which refers to the choicest of horses that usually came from Egypt. These horses had a hidden beauty and strength to them. Their beauty was not always realized until they started to show their power in wars or parades. She could see how such a description fit her. Even though her beauty was covered by worldly toil and activities, it was still there ready to come out in the right environment. She also realized she had also done much in her power to accomplish the tasks set before her by others, but there was another aspect of the horse that described her and that had to do with its swiftness. The king had recognized her swiftness to seek and pursue him.[38]

He was not done describing her beauty. The horse described her hidden beauty, ever ready to come forth in the right setting, but her cheeks spoke of her natural beauty. In her culture the cheeks were highly considered when it came to estimating the natural beauty of a woman, and highlighting them in the right way was important. It was clear the king recognized the natural endowment of her beauty in spite of the influence of the world upon her.

The king also noted how her braided hair appeared to be as rows of jewels to him. He was acknowledging that her hair was also highlighting her beauty, while symbolizing her strength to maintain a steady pose.

---

[37] Song of Solomon 1:8
[38] The description of the Shulamite girl is found in Song of Solomon 1:9-11

49

The Shulamite girl was also reminded how precious jewels possess their own glory, and in her culture the hair served as the woman's glory.[39]

He noted her neck as being adorned with chains of gold. She was quite aware that the neck didn't seem all that important to others, but Yahweh pointed out how stiff-necked people refuse to humble themselves before Him, and that all will eventually come under some type of yoke, whether it be the light yoke of His love or the heavy yoke of sin. For a neck to be adorned with gold, it must be one that can bend in humility to receive such divine gifts of grace. A neck adorned with chains also reveals a natural gentleness that will manifest itself in meekness, as well as a controlled strength that will be properly trained and disciplined.

After the king described her, he revealed his plans for her. He will make her borders of gold. Gold pointed to that which possesses divine characteristics. It is clear that all lasting beauty is a matter of Yahweh's artistic work in the life of His people. Man may display beauty, but it is surface and is described as fading glory, but when the Creator does such work, it is in reference to inner character whose glory will be unmasked through a person's countenance.

The monarch talked about studs of silver. Silver carried so much meaning to her people because it was always used in relationship to redemption. Redemption held all matters together for the Jewish people. They had been redeemed from Egypt by Yahweh, and it was silver brackets that held the studs up in the tabernacle. It was with a silver shekel that all male souls were to be redeemed before any king could number them. King David was reminded of this very fact when he was provoked by an unseen entity to number the people before redeeming every male, bringing a plague on the people of Israel.[40]

It was clear to her that the king was talking about her redemption. He was going to ransom her from the claims of others, actually buying her to take her out of her present state to establish her in his royal household. At that time, she would be prepared to take her place in his kingdom, clothed in royal garments, and established to sit beside him.

---

[39] 1 Corinthians 11:15,16
[40] Exodus 26:19-25; 30:11-16; 2 Samuel 24, note verse 24; 1 Chronicles 21:1

She rejoiced over his invitation and was overwhelmed by his description of her. The fact that he had it in his heart to bring her to himself in a personal, intimate way, set her own spirit free in a way that she couldn't have imagined. Beauty that had been hidden and caged was now unveiling itself in her love for him, sending forth a beautiful fragrance that filled the air with sweetness. It was her own special sacrifice, for no one else would be able to smell or appreciate the fragrance of her love like the king.

It was her turn to put into words how she saw her king.[41] He had become a bundle of myrrh, a substance used in the anointing oil in the tabernacle in relationship to sacrifices, kings, and priests.[42] Real love will often come out of suffering and sacrifice that expresses itself in humility.

Myrrh was also used for purification, used in cosmetics and as a stimulant. It let off a strong odor, and the anointing fragrance of her king's love was overwhelming to her as it satisfied her inner being with strong assurance. Her encounter with him made it clear that he had opened the way for her to be purified and to be clothed in unspeakable beauty, knowing that he offered the very healing balm to her weary soul that would bring restoration to her inner being.

There only was one term she could use, "my well-beloved." She would simply drop it to, "my beloved" in due time to express her affections towards him but the word, "well," was so important. It pointed to a love that was bubbling beneath the surface, ready to break forth in some expressive form that would serve as a token of their relationship.

It was clear that he now possessed her heart, but real love must be maintained between pillars of discipline. It must not swing from flimsy branches of fickle sentiment and fanciful notions. There are important pillars that must be erected to keep love stable. These pillars will balance each other out as well, such as faith and grace, mercy and judgment, trust and obedience, and spirit and truth to name a few; but they must be in place to protect the integrity of her love for him.

---

[41] The Shulamite girl's description of the king is found in Song of Solomon 1:13,14
[42] Exodus 30:22-32

She clearly wanted to protect her love for him in every way possible for he reminded her of a cluster of camphire, which was comprised of henna-flowers that were used by handmaidens as an exterior adornment. Her placement of henna-flowers at Engedi where grapes grew would be a most unusual sight for those who understood the terrain, but for her that is how she saw her beloved. His love clearly adorned him and made him stand out as one who could never again fit in a common place.[43]

The Shulamite girl's description of the king caused him to respond to her. "Behold, thou art fair, my love; behold, thou art fair; thou hast doves' eyes."[44] There is that word again, "fair," being used twice, serving as a witness before heaven. The king was not only reaffirming that she was beautiful to him, but he now was saying she has the eyes of a dove. That statement made her realize that no longer were her eyes glancing at the world and wandering in uncertainty, but now they had become single in their focus towards the king.[45]

It was her desire, not only for him to possess her heart, but for her to come to a place where she only had eyes for her king. She could do nothing less than respond to him. "Behold, thou art fair, my beloved, yea, pleasant; also our bed is green. The beams of our house are cedar, and our rafters of fir."[46] Her beloved possessed such beauty that it was a delight to her, as well as those who experienced it, producing an abundance of sustaining fruit that brought life and purpose to her. It was clear that his character was like the tall cedars that housed integrity, pointing to right standing before heaven, held up by the cypress, firs that were found in graveyards, which points to death to the old way to give way for the new to be established. She realized she could no longer look back to the old for it was behind her, she must look forward to a new life in the presence of her king.

The king then introduced himself in a different way. He had invited her to his chamber to sit at his table. There they spoke of what they

---

[43] Song of Songs, Watchman Nee, © 1965 by Christian Literature Crusade, pg. 32
[44] Song of Solomon 1:15
[45] Ephesians 6:5-7
[46] Song of Solomon 1:16,17

perceived about one another. Each unveiling of their feelings allowed him to bring her to a place where he could now introduce himself to her more intimately. "I AM the rose of Sharon, and the lily of the valleys."[47]

She was reminded of Yahweh intruding into Moses' reality and introducing Himself as the, "I AM THAT I AM." The concept of "I AM" had to do with Yahweh always being, will be today, and will be tomorrow. No one can be "I AM" except that which houses the divine. As the rose of Sharon, he might be regarded as insignificant by those who fail to see him for who he is, but he is the abiding fragrance that can only be captured or savored by those who are close enough to receive and enjoy the beautiful fragrance of his life.[48]

The king stressed to her that he is the lone lily of the valleys, one of the first spring flowers to rise up in the midst of what appears to be a lifeless, undesirable environment. He would abide among the thorns so that his love could be made available to others.[49] It was clear that he was implying that those who might follow him into thorny places may experience loneliness and piercing in such an environment.

The Shulamite girl realized that she wanted to be where the king abided. He may be a lily among thorns but she saw him as an apple tree among the trees of the wood. It was her way of making a very important connection and distinction. She knew that God considered the Law and the Jewish people the apple of His eye.[50]

In Hebrew the pupil of the eye is expressed as "the daughter of the eye."[51] The Shulamite girl realize that the eye is precious, tender, and carefully guarded, which points to God's holy Law and her people being guarded and protected by Yahweh. She wanted the king to hold such a place in her life, but she also knew that the apple tree would point the king to the citron tree.[52]

---

[47] Song of Solomon 2:1
[48] Exodus 3:14; 2 Corinthians 2:15-16
[49] Song of Solomon 2:2; Romans 11:16
[50] Deuteronomy 32:10; Psalm 17:8
[51] Psalms, A Devotional Commentary, Herbert Lockyer, Sr., © 1992 by Kregel Publications, pg. 36
[52] Song of Solomon 2:3

The citron tree was unique in that it has a lovely foliage whose leaves do not fall in winter.[53] It was clear that like the tree, the king's love would never waver during challenging seasons. The fruit of the tree has a similar appearance as the pomegranate, but tastes like a tangerine with a touch of lemon. It was considered a "golden fruit" because of its rare fragrance. The use of this fruit to describe him, told the king that he clearly stood out among all others to her, and she took comfort that in his shadow she could find rest as she deeply breathed in His fragrance and tasted the sweetness of His love.

It was clear that she had become so caught up with the ecstasy of experiencing his love that she failed to notice that the present world had clearly faded. As she began to once again sense her seat at his beautiful banqueting table, she had to shake off her reluctance to remember where she was. As she settled back in her chair to enjoy her king's presence and partake of the wondrous dainties at the banquet table, she noted the bold ensign that appeared to envelope the room. Silently she began to repeat what was written on it, "And his banner over me was love."[54]

Officially Introduced
(The Second Companion)

The former slave girl sat at a large table fit for a king. She felt out of place. She was somewhat cleaned up but still felt dirty inside and unsure of her situation. In the past she knew her place. She had, in fact, been demoted various times in her master's house until she became nothing more than mere kitchen help, and when all was said and done, she was left with crumbs that were inedible, but regardless of the demotions, she always knew her place.

The food on the table looked grand to her and her mouth watered, but she wasn't sure if she could partake of it without losing it the minute

[53] Song of Songs, Watchman Nee, © 1965 by Christian Literature Crusade, pgs. 36, 37
[54] Song of Solomon 2:4

it touched her stomach. It was clear she was not prepared to sit at the table, let alone partake of its bounty.

The king entered the room. Since she didn't really know her place, she did not know whether to stand and bow or nod her head in acknowledgment of him. In the marketplace he appeared to be a business man seeking out something of value that had been lost, but in the banqueting room he was the master and in her mind, she was nothing more than a mere, worthless servant that was not only out of place at his table, but clearly didn't belong in his house, in the banqueting room, or in his presence.

He smiled and nodded at her, confirming that there was no action required on her part towards him. He sat in his chair at the head of the table and looked at her with eyes that seemed to flood her soul with warmth. She sensed he could see the barrenness of her soul and the leanness of her spirit without judging her.

"Are you not hungry?" he asked.

She smiled. "This truly is fit for a queen, but if you knew my diet, you would understand all of this food is a bit overwhelming. It's rich and I'm sure satisfying, but I'm not certain I could partake of it at this time."

He smiled and reached for some milk and bread. "Surely, you can handle a bit of milk, and you can dip the bread in it."[55]

He broke a couple of pieces of bread off and handed one to her. "Let us partake together." They both dipped their bread at the same time and put it in their mouths. It was clear that unlike the coarse bread of slavery, this bread had substance and it easily enough went down with the milk. She realized the milk was pure and the bread sweet to the taste and satisfying to her soul.

He quietly sat back to carefully examine every move she made.

"You have questions, feel free to ask them."

She was surprised that he brought up such a proposal. She had been conditioned to be a slave from birth and programed to obey. As one born into slavery, she had no rights to personal opinions or questions. She was told to do be dutiful in all matters concerning the

---

[55] John 6:35; 1 Peter 2:1-3

household and expected to carry out all that was required of her without comment.

She had been studying him to see if he was trustworthy, and realized that she would first have to test his intention by simply being honest. After all, what did she have to lose? She swallowed hard before committing herself. "Why me?" she asked.

"Why not?" he answered.

"I'm a slave among many who stood on that auction block. I have prostituted myself and been prostituted by my masters. I do not deserve your attention and kindness," she answered.

"Where are your accusers?" he asked.[56]

She looked down and slightly shook her head to acknowledge there were none.

"You have been redeemed, purchased, and pardoned," he answered, "but you must believe it is so and receive it into your heart to know and experience the forgiveness that is attached to it."[57]

She looked at him, "I may appear clean, but it is only outward because in my mind I'm a slave to the damned, and within I'm dirty, utterly filthy, and unworthy of any other type of consideration from such a benevolent Lord as yourself."[58]

His stare remained kind but penetrated her soul. "You can let the past define you or you can believe that you have been cleansed through redemption and your worthiness is found in who I am and my work on your behalf."[59]

She shook her head as if to say "No." Tears began to make their entrance. "I'm nothing but a rejected, lost lamb among many that couldn't find my way through the great darkness that was upon my soul."

The smile that broke out on his face was reassuring. "I am the good shepherd who seeks out the lost lambs who are crying out in the darkness."[60]   Struggling to hold back sobs, she asked, "How do you

---

[56] John 8:9-11
[57] 2 Samuel 4:9; Ephesians 1:7; 1 Peter 1:18,19; Revelation 5:9
[58] Isaiah 64:6
[59] 1 Corinthians 1:30
[60] Luke 15:4-7; John 10:11

know whether I was crying or not, for my cries have been silent, a matter of the heart."

He smiled, "Have you not cried to your Creator, asking that He meet you in your plight by delivering you from your miserable state?"

She became confused by his insight and let out a sigh. "It's true that I cried out to the unknown, to one who is called God to provide the solution, but I felt my cries being swallowed by the nothingness of the vastness that was before me, and therefore, expected nothing."

"Do you not believe that the God who made the vastness of the universe could provide you with a solution?" he asked.

She thought for a moment before she carefully spoke. "As Creator of the universe, He could provide the solution if it pleased Him to do so, but why would He concern Himself with me?"

He leaned forward and took her hands in his. This time she felt his look penetrating every barrier erected in her soul, causing them to collapse. The words he spoke made her heart skip a beat. "Because as Creator He loves His creation, especially mankind."[61]

"How could a Holy God look my way, even if He loved me?"

"As Creator, He sees your potential, not who you have become because of the world, but what you can become."

"If that is true, why have I not seen the answer to the solution to my plight?" she asked.

"How would you know what to look for?"

His question caused her to pause and meditate on what he asked. He proceeded to answer the question, "You could not know what you were asking for, looking for, and quietly seeking in the midst of utter hopelessness."

She shook her head in agreement. He then made a simple, but powerful statement that shook her very being with excitement and expectation. "I am HE, the one you have been looking for."[62]

---

[61] John 3:16
[62] John 4:22-26

Faltering Love

Learning to Hear

I found myself feeling very uncomfortable at Jesus' table. I knew that He invited me to come and sit awhile and learn of Him, but I was somewhat shocked at the feelings I had about being in His presence. I knew the foundational teachings of Scripture, and had taken pride in the fact I could hold my own in Scriptural debate, but debate is considered one of the workings of sin.[1] My conceit allowed me to assume that I knew what I needed to believe, but sitting at the table of Jesus made me feel undone, uncertain, and at times apprehensive.

It was at the table of Jesus that I realized I had originally set up the servings I partook of on my personal table of religious notions. I had sought knowledge of Him, but failed to seek Him. At His table, I had to face the reality that I didn't know Him in a personal way, and what notions were left were quickly dissipating, leaving me with a leanness in my spirit.

I was also struggling with the fact that the voice I heard in the beginning of my Christian life had grown eerily quiet. I knew the written Word served as God's voice, but in my present state, it lacked inspiration and had become silent. I struggled within myself. Even though Jesus was closer, He still seemed far away. I knew the distance was not His doing but my doing.

It was at His table that the Lord revealed what I had done with His Word. Hebrews 4:12 states that the Word is sharper than any two-edged sword revealing the motives and intentions of the heart. Instead of allowing the sword to dissect me to reveal my inner character, I had dissected the sword, and it lay before me in pieces. The handle lay to the side, the blade was in fragments and had become tarnished as well as dull. The Lord even asked me if the Word in its present state could possibly have any real impact on my life. I realized that in my search to

---

[1] Romans 1:29; Titus 3:9

appease my religious notions, I had rendered the most powerful weapon useless.

The Lord was gracious enough to give me a choice. Did I want His sword to remain useless or did I want Him to put it back together for the purpose of impacting my life with it? To me the choice was obvious. I asked Him to put it back together and use it on me however He saw fit. I watched Him as He masterfully put the sword back together. He brought the luster out on the handle, wiped off the tarnish, and sharpened the blade. The next thing He did was take it and thrust it into my midsection and when He did, I felt blinders falling from my eyes.

In Matthew 13:13-15, Jesus spoke of the prophecy in Isaiah 6:9 and 10 which stated that the people would hear but not understand, see but not perceive what they were looking at for their hearts had waxed gross, their ears had become dull of hearing, and their eyes closed to the truth, preventing them from being truly converted. As I considered the implications behind the Scriptures, I realized I had not been truly converted to true righteousness. I had a zeal for God, but I was ignorant of what constituted God's righteousness. As a result, I went about establishing my own righteousness.[2]

Since I had a high opinion of my idea of righteousness, I became self-righteous and judgmental towards others who didn't see it my way. I was looking at everything through a perverted prism. It was at the table that the Lord revealed to me that in my self-righteousness I had often judged Him as not being righteous and just. In fact, I was judging what He was doing in other people's lives instead of discerning that He was missing in my activities.

I started shaking inside. I had judged the righteous Judge of all. I realized how foolish I had become. The Lord had given me a new heart, but it had never been truly circumcised by His Word. He gave me the eyes of faith to see, but I never exercised them because I trusted in what I perceived on an intellectual level and not on what the Word needed to reveal about Jesus. I was given ears to hear, but I never learned to

---

[2] Romans 10:2,3

discern the voice of His Holy Spirit in the midst of all the other predominate voices around me.[3]

And, what about that zealous love I started out with? Well, it had truly faltered. In fact, it never really got completely out of the gate. As soon as the door opened for me to be part of the race, my initial love fell flat on its face as I redirected my zeal to chase after some religious notion about what I thought Christianity was all about. However, I was void of any real understanding that Christianity was not about my religious best but about establishing the life of Christ in me so I could be identified to Him.

Each new revelation about my great failure made me want to either hide from Him or run from His table, but in my mind, there was no turning back. I had already unintentionally turned away from Him and out of grace and mercy He came after me and once again sent forth the invitation for me to rise up and follow Him to a place of fellowship--to His table.[4] It was clear that He was the one who always had to invite and pursue after me. In my initially lost state He found me, in my wandering state He came after me, and in my desperate state He reached His hand out to me in order to lead me to a place of restoration.

At Jesus' table, I realized I was to be served by the Spirit of the Lord. The Scriptures would be imparted to me a bit at a time until I was able to chew on them without choking on the meat that had been carefully prepared. It was true that I had been drinking the milk of doctrine, while occasionally mixing a bit of the bread of revelation of Christ in it, making it milk toast, but I had never developed the teeth to properly break down the Word. I had to come to the place where I could chew the meat enough so that I could swallow it in order to assimilate it for spiritual nourishment. Without properly chewing the meat of the Word, I would never gain the ability to discern between good and evil in order to bring about spiritual growth which would enable me to do the will of God.[5]

---

[3] Deuteronomy 30:6 refer to Colossians 2:11; Ezekiel 36:25-27 refer to Hebrews 10:16;
  2 Corinthians 5:7; Proverbs 8:34; Hebrews 11:6
[4] Revelation 3:20
[5] John 4:32-34; Romans 12:1-2; 1 Corinthians 2:10-14; Hebrews 5:12-14

I was a bit shocked at my predicament. It was clear that knowledge alone about Scripture was not enough and having theology did not mean I was necessarily grounded on the right foundation.[6] It was at Jesus' table I realized that I had been conditioned a certain way in order to be indoctrinated in schools of thought that would determine how I interpreted Scriptures.

This uninspired man-centered frame of reference was causing me to see Jesus in an abstract manner. Granted, I saw certain points about Jesus, but for the most part, it was not clear or complete. I didn't realize my perception of Him was not only a type of wall that kept Him at a distance, but it kept me from seeing who He was. As a result, at different times His motives were brought into question, His ways into scrutiny, and His judgments ignored as I bowed before what I thought I understood about Him.

The revelation that caused the biggest shock to all to my senses was the harsh reality that my mind had not been transformed. I was saved out of a cult but I didn't realize that the cult was not completely rooted out of me. I had unknowingly operated on assumed beliefs that fit into my latest conclusions about certain religious matters. Once I concluded that something was correct it became a presumption. I failed to see that assumed beliefs belong to others and presumptions became strong opinions, but none of it necessarily had anything to do with truth.[7]

We can do nothing against the truth, but if we do not believe and own a truth for ourselves, it will have no real authority in our life. Without such authority, we will not be able to give an account of what we believe to others.[8] In fact, without authority, we can be turned into spiritual pretzels that will leave us confused about what we do believe and what is really true.

The Bible was clear that I was to come out and be separate from the world but I still possessed a worldly attitude.[9] I was to live a spiritual life in the heights of heaven, but the reality was, I was living a fleshly life in

---

[6] 1 Corinthians 8:1,2
[7] Philippians 2:5; Romans 12:1,2; Ephesians 4:22-24; 2 Peter 2:10
[8] 2 Corinthians 13:8; 1 Peter 3:15
[9] 2 Corinthians 6:14-18

the dregs of guilt and shame. I was called to live a victorious, overcoming life, but I was being overcome by defeat and despair. I had exposed myself to the religion of man and not to the glory of Christ.

I remember that the Holy Spirit started out slowly imparting revelation to me. He began with the Beatitudes in Matthew 5:1-12.[10] I have always appreciated the beauty of the Beatitudes, but I never really stopped to consider whether I possessed such attitudes.

Attitudes are of the upmost importance in the Christian life because they determine how you will approach something. I never realized that in the kingdom of God the right approach was everything. In fact, if you do not start with the right approach, you will completely miss the target.

As the Holy Spirit begin to unveil the simplicity of the Beatitudes to my spirit, the more profound they became. I found myself meditating on them in ways that made me feel overwhelmed by their meanings. It was clear that I did not possess the right attitude. For instance, I never approached the truths of God like a cringing beggar, humbled and trembling, and even though I was miserable with guilt and desperate because of my hopeless plight, I was never completely broken over my sin to the point I mourned because of what it did to God, my relationship to Him, and to others. I was self-sufficient instead of meek, hungry for knowledge but not thirsty for righteousness, judgmental instead of merciful, deluded instead of pure, and a self-serving servant instead of a child of God.

Each unveiling of my attitude revealed that I was like an onion, covered with various layers of skin. Each time the Holy Spirit peeled back a layer to reveal my attitude, the more of the rottenness of the attitude of the "old man" in me was being exposed. It proved to be bittersweet. It was bitter in the sense that it was such a stench and embarrassment to my spirit, but sweet because it began to set my soul free to experience the living revelation that had been veiled from my intellectual understanding.

Even though the Holy Spirit was gentle in His impartation to me, I became aware that a revolution was taking place in my soul. Although I often felt undone in the Lord's presence, I also had a sense that much

---

[10] Ephesians 1:17-19

work was being done in me. In many ways it was dreadful, yet awesome at the same time, sobering but exciting, disturbing nevertheless transforming, and overwhelming but yet exhilarating.[11]

I wasn't sure where my table experience would lead me, but the one reality was my growing awareness that I would not come away from the table the same person. Some changes taking place were obvious, while others were subtle, but the one fact I became cognizant of was that I could never let such a great rift take place between Jesus and me again.

Although I was sitting at His table, I became keenly aware that I was becoming more desperate for Him. I was growing in the knowledge of Him, and the more that was unveiled to my heart the more I wanted to be closer to Him. However, I had to first hear what the Spirit was saying before I could be brought into a more intimate relationship with my Lord. My soul became restless causing me to realize that I must never settle for less when it came to my life in Jesus. I understood that I needed to see Him and the more He was unveiled to my spirit, the more I would know Him. It was clear I needed to know the person of Jesus in greater measure to understand His wondrous character and obtain a bigger sense of His great work of redemption on my behalf. The more I understood the different facets of His character, ways and work, the more I found myself in a deeper place of humility.[12]

The Lattice

The Shulamite girl's experience with the king was glorious. The revelation she had received up front during her time at his banqueting table was exhilarating as well as humbling. She had rested in his love, while feeling his abiding protection and strength in her life. She had recognized the need to respect such love and as a result she had kept others from disturbing their time together, but life goes on and worldly demands and responsibilities never cease, causing her to once again return to the daily activities of the world.[13]

---

[11] Philippians 1:6
[12] Philippians 3:7,8; 2 Peter 1:3-10
[13] Song of Solomon 2:5-7

In her culture a dowry was required and the man must prepare the place for his betrothed and receive his father's approval that their abode was ready before they could live together as husband and wife. In the eyes of her culture they were already married, but meanwhile life goes on in her mother's home, allowing, not only a time of preparation for both, but one of discovery.[14]

The initial feelings she had for the king had caused joy to abound in her spirit but as the current of life continued, the zeal began to fade away. She returned to her life in the vineyard and was once again settling into a routine.

To her surprise, she heard the voice of her beloved in the distance. She would know his voice anywhere and she sensed his joy in coming to her. There was a lightness in his steps that would not allow any hindrance or obstacles to impede his pace. But, instead of joy springing up within her as she saw him in the distance, she found herself feeling unsure.[15] Granted, she had a glorious experience with him the first time, which left her with sentimental memories, but sentiment is fickle and memories can set one up to be disappointed if expectations on both sides are not met.

She realized there had been enough time and space between them that she couldn't be sure of his feelings and she was unsure of her reactions. Why was her new love faltering for one who proved to be so trustworthy? She thought of him as her beloved, but it was becoming clear to her that her love for him was as unstable as waves on the ocean. Her new love had no real anchor to hold it in place.[16] She found herself stepping behind a lattice to observe him from a distance in order to calculate how she would respond.

As the Shulamite girl took her place behind the lattice, she became aware of him watching her from behind a wall, looking towards the windows as if waiting for an invitation from her to come closer so they could commune together. She wrestled with why she was so unsettled about meeting him. She had so valued their first time together but now

---

[14] Matthew 1:18-25; Luke 1:27-34; John 14:1-3
[15] Song of Solomon 2:8,9; John 10:3-5
[16] Ephesian 4:14

she felt shyness, fear, and trepidation. Before, he had invited her to his chambers, but now he was on her turf. Their first meeting revealed her occupation in the world, but this was her home, and it was capable of revealing more of her character.

The girl realized she had her ideas and memories of the king based on their first meeting, but he was not coming to her as a king but as a shepherd. A king invites but a shepherd leads.[17] She had no problem in accepting the king's invitation to come to his chambers and sit at his banqueting table, but the idea of possibly letting him into her personal life to see if she was prepared to go further into their relationship by following him into the unknown was somewhat unnerving to her.

She quietly chided herself for what she could plainly see as her silliness. In her mind, she had just become comfortable with him being a king, and she knew her anxiety over meeting him as a shepherd was unwarranted. Every great leader learns to lead before they can rule. He may have come to her as a benevolent ruler the first time, but now she had to learn to follow him as a good shepherd.

As she wrestled with herself over her foolishness, his voice penetrated through her mental conflict. "Rise up, my love, my fair one, and come away."[18] He was confirming that his feelings for her had not changed. She was still beautiful to him and he still loved her, and then she realized how simple the invitation was. She was to rise up out of her present situation and follow him.

After his invitation he spoke of the dormant winter season passing where their love was concerned, and that it was presently spring where regeneration was coming forth, expressing new, vibrant life. When he mentioned the green figs, she was reminded that the green figs remained so through the winter, and that even though their love had been challenged by the winter, it had endured.[19] She realized that true love must withstand different seasons, and for theirs it was a type of winter that revealed some trials and challenges. It was not that her love for him had grown cold, but the obstacles and demands of the world had

---

[17] Song of Solomon 2:10
[18] Ibid
[19] Song of Solomon 2:11-13

caused it to become dormant and it needed to be revived. It is true her infant love had faltered, but it was ready to come out in a new way. In fact, it had the potential to produce fruits.

The invitation came again, "Arise, my love, my fair one, and come away."[20] The Shulamite girl realized that if her love for her beloved was to reach beyond the dormant season, she had to follow him into a new season. In her heart she wanted to follow, but she was still hesitant because she realized the lattice represented her limited perception and the wall revealed her uncertainty when it came to the depth of her commitment. It was becoming obvious that the wall of speculation and uncertainty was still present and remained between them.

The truth is, she didn't want to look through a lattice that caused an abstract perspective of him, or at him with a wall in-between that prevented him from revealing himself to her, or through windows that clouded their view of each other. There was only one thing she could do and that was to admit her struggles. "O my dove, that art in the clefts of the rock, in the secret places of the stairs, let me see thy countenance, let me hear thy voice; for sweet is thy voice, and thy countenance is comely."[21]

The Shulamite girl knew that her beloved's focus was for and on her, but she admitted that although he may see her, he had become mysterious to her. She remembered that Moses was placed upon a rock, hidden in the cleft of the rock, and covered by the hand of God until Yahweh's glory and back parts passed by.[22] Her beloved's glory as king had clearly been shrouded by the cleft of the rock and he had been hidden away and prepared in secret places that were unknown to her. That is when she asked him to let her see his glory and hear his voice, for she knew she would recognize the sweetness of his voice and the beauty of his countenance.[23]

It was then she also admitted that the foxes of the world and the little foxes of the old life had caused much damage, resulting in her love for

---

[20] Song of Solomon 2:13
[21] Song of Solomon 2:14
[22] Exodus 33:18-23
[23] Song of Solomon 2:14

him faltering, but she also acknowledged that there were vines that still had tender grapes that could bring forth needed fruit to ensure not only a new season for their love to grow, but to be established.[24]

She did not know how much of her immature love was left that could be revived, but she knew as soon as day broke, it would reveal that not all was lost when it came to her vineyard or her love for him.[25]

The Wrestling Match
(The Second Companion)

The slave girl greatly enjoyed her time sitting at the table with her Lord. He had answered many questions. She knew his answers were true, but she still struggled with the memories and accusations of the past. Her new Lord had assured her that she was accepted as a beloved one at his table, but she still felt unlovable.[26]

She had dreamed of being at such a table and longed to have a relationship just like the one she was experiencing with her Lord, but now that it was happening, she was uncertain of what to do. It was all so foreign to her. What was she to do or expect in this new relationship? She could revert back and simply step out and operate according to former practices, but she realized that her place had changed and the past was behind her. She had found security at the table with the one who had redeemed her, but when she was alone with her thoughts, she quickly became insecure.

The Lord had other business to attend to, not only in his household, but in his kingdom, and had left her with trustworthy aids that required some personal disciplines on her part. To some extent the aids helped her to develop a routine, but, in his absence, it became obvious that she was still vulnerable. She had a new life before her, but it was clear some of the aspects of her old life was still very much in place, clinging to her like graveclothes. She realized that the same suspicious attitude she

---

[24] Song of Solomon 2:15
[25] Song of Solomon 2:16
[26] Ephesians 1:6,7

had before might crop up when she least expected. She found the longer she was apart from the Lord, the more her suspicions resurrected barriers, creating a type of unseen cage around her emotions.[27] Even though he had captured her heart with his love and kindness, she was still floundering when it came to her love and level of commitment towards him.

It was clear that his love had overwhelmed her, but she became aware that the zeal she felt in her love towards him had greatly fluctuated because it was based on sentiment that could easily be hampered and dimmed by the right circumstances. She realized that she felt the most secure in the presence of her Lord, but such dependency was not healthy. In real love, a person doesn't need to be present at all times for love to be confirmed or secured. It concerned her that her love had no legs to simply stand and trust in the love that her Lord had already shown to her.

As she thought about it, she felt foolish. Why could she not simply accept the love of this wonderful man? Why did she revert back to the old worldly attitude towards such matters when it had created such despair in her in the past? There were so many times it left her hopeless, yet she seemed to be drawn back to her old life by some sick promise that she was missing something that would prove to be more satisfying than what she had. She knew it was all nonsense but her appetites for temporary satisfaction proved to be overpowering at times.[28]

If that temptation wasn't enough, she was wrestling with the fact she could have the best of both worlds if she was willing to compromise here, play the game there, and use her new position in the household to secure aspects of the world that had been an attraction to her in the past. As she wrestled with such notions, she realized the folly of such reasoning. After all, her Lord had delivered her from her past so she could have a new life in the present and hope in the future. She clearly couldn't successfully live a double life in which one deserved her complete love and adoration while the other one would require her very soul. She could see that she would eventually be forced to make a

---

[27] Isaiah 26:3; 2 Corinthians 10:3-6; Ephesians 6:11, 17; Philippians 4:6-9
[28] Romans 5:1-5; 1 John 4:19

decision as to who she would ultimately pursue, love, and serve.[29] Realistically, she knew that the present love she had towards her Lord would eventually falter at such nagging temptations if she kept giving them an audience.

Here she was a former slave who now had it all, but she was missing what was necessary and important to go forward. Even though she was surrounded by beauty, it seemed hollow. She could freely sit at the banqueting table that offered much, but the excitement and expectation that she initially had was absent. She had such great promises before her, yet there was some type of leanness growing in her spirit. She possessed that which was satisfying, yet she was becoming a restless wave, ready to be driven anywhere that would lead her away from her inner struggle.[30]

She was obviously at some type of crossroad and very confused about it. She still possessed a worldly mindset and a carnal attitude about life, and still viewed her creator and life from this tainted premise. Both were serving as strongholds in her mind, contaminating what she saw, perverting what she heard, and hindering her from seeing what was trustworthy. Ultimately, it not only prevented her from discerning what was real, but kept her from the freedom to receive what was true.[31]

As she wrestled with what seemed to be endless drudgery in her present life and stagnation in her soul, she heard the voice of the one who loved her. She knew it was the Lord's voice, but there was a different tone to it. It was not a demanding or commanding voice, rather it was a voice calling to her to come away from the table and follow his leading.

It was a bit confusing to her. Why didn't he come to her as he had before? The twilight of the day was upon them and the changing of the season was making an entrance upon the terrain. She may have been restless in her soul, but she had grown accustomed to where she was in regard to her position in his household.[32] The idea of leaving the

---

[29] Matthew 6:21-24
[30] Galatians 5:16-18
[31] Romans 8:5-9; 1 Corinthians 2:10-14; 3:1-3; 2 Corinthians 6:14-18; 10:3-5; James 4:4; 1 John 2:15-17
[32] Matthew 16:24

71

familiar to follow the leading of his voice into the twilight of the unknown was a bit unnerving. After all, what would he require of her, and would she be properly prepared to face the new season that was upon them?

Her hesitation to respond caused him to call her once again to follow him. She suddenly realized that her soul had been seeking change and that she was close to casting the familiar aside to chase after what she had known, but now she was reluctant to fling aside the familiar to follow after the one who redeemed her. She could see that inconsistency was still very much a part of her character.

The former slave girl suddenly came face-to-face with her foolishness. She may had been restless enough to toy with the idea of roaming in the world, but she wasn't prepared to follow the one she loved into the unknown. She voiced her concern in his direction, asking if it wouldn't be better for both of them to wait for the sunrise to bring clarity to the day and the landscape.

Suddenly, she sensed that he had simply departed. He had intruded into her wrestling match enough to disrupt the inner conflict she was having, only to create another one that brought fear to her that was already graduating into guilt and shame due to her failure to respond. She was now left alone to face the harsh reality of what was really missing in her life. She was shocked to realize that it was convicting love towards her Lord that was lacking, leaving her insecure. Her love had no real substance to sustain her, for it lacked the character to endure the testing that comes in the twilight of such relationships, ultimately proving to be self-serving when invited to venture into new territory.

She knew in her heart that if her love towards her Lord had been true and pure, the time or season wouldn't have mattered, and she would have flung all aside upon hearing his voice the first time in order to be with him, to be at his side, and to be willing to follow him into the darkness.

An Empty Chair

Sitting at the table with Jesus made me alert as to how personal He was when it came to my life. I was also aware that His eye was on me, ever regarding the work being done in my life. There were a couple of times that I sensed there was someone else at His side and that He was viewing me from a side angle while sharing something intimate with the person talking to Him.

I had to admit to myself that learning of Jesus was far better than learning about Him. He had been far from me, but now He was being brought ever closer to my heart. Each new revelation of Him brought Him out of the barren wilderness of my understanding, enabling me to see He was alive, real, and worth knowing. As He became illuminated to me, He was being transported out of the darkness of ignorance based on assumptions and presumptions. I was learning the intent and principles behind His teachings that were giving me insight into His heart attitude about all matters pertaining to life and godliness.[33] Some of the things I was learning caused such excitement in me I wanted other people to taste it. It was as if the knowledge was overflowing the banks of my soul and I knew I had to share what I was learning in order to make room for more revelation.

I found myself always looking for the opportunity to share with others what I had experienced at the Jesus' table. Most were receptive to what I shared, but there were a few who became very critical of me. In spite of a few negative responses, I went back to the table, confident that the Holy Spirit would share more with me.

Eventually, it began to dawn on me that my sharing was more for my benefit. It was not that I was zealous or a big mouth, it was that I selfishly wanted more for myself and that I desperately needed it to fill the vacant places left by my former religious pursuits. Since I could not receive more until I imparted my latest revelation to someone else, I was quite motivated to share the joy His Word was bringing to my soul each day as opportunities were presented to me.

---

[33] 2 Peter 1:3,4

Joy of His Word not only caused me to want to share the priceless nuggets I received at His table, but it was becoming an anchor in my soul. It was steadying my spirit as my soul was being enlarged to ever look up and learn what it would mean to soar above the limited perspective of this world to gain the heavenly perspective of the Lord.[34]

At such times I realized that I was beginning to covet a closer relationship with Him, but I knew I had to wait to be invited to come closer, and that at present I was in the right chair, seated at the right position at His table. I continued to remind myself I had to learn of Him first before I could come closer to Him and be entrusted with those things that were close to His heart.

Clearly, He knew what was important to me, but I didn't really know what was important to Him outside of doctrine and theology. It was becoming increasingly obvious to me that our relationship had been one-sided. He was ever aware of me, trying to get my attention, change my direction, and bring me to a higher place in Him and I was out doing my own thing. Granted, it was religious and I was into His Word, but my personal life was missing the mark of the high calling I had in Him. I had failed to come to a greater knowledge of my Lord, preventing me from entering the door of sweet fellowship, rendering what I understood to become dead-letter and ineffective.[35]

One day I was sitting at the table of fellowship and I heard His voice calling out to me. I remember turning towards it in expectation. I will never forget what happened. He instructed me to go out and share what I had learned at His table. I sat there wondering what to do. What was I to share and with who?

Peace settled in my spirit. I didn't know how it would happen, but I sensed He somehow had already set it up. I had to simply knock on the door and trust Him to open or close the right door.[36] Surprisingly, the first door I knocked on opened up to me. I was allowed to speak to the women's group of the church I was attending. I knew all the women and felt comfortable for the most part, but I had a bit of trepidation about

---

[34] Job 39:27-29; Ephesians 2:6
[35] Luke 14:7-11; Romans 7:6; 2 Corinthians 3:6
[36] Matthew 7:7,8; Revelation 3:7

whether I could effectively deliver the message that was burning in my heart.

In my mind, my one consolation was that there probably would not be very many women present so if I flopped too badly, they would most likely give me a pass and encourage me in some kind way. To make an interesting story concise, the place was packed and some of the women were sitting in an adjacent room. I prayed silently and gave it to the Lord and when I stood up to speak the message that was on my heart, I felt peace surround me, and as I began to speak His presence enfolded me. The room was so quiet that I could have heard a pin drop as I shared what I had learned. There was an authority in the message I had never seen, and a power that I had never felt before. I later learned that authority and power in the midst of the Lord's presence represents anointing.

I was awestruck at how the words coming forth were sharp, penetrating hearts and minds. It seemed that some were at awe, others were being awakened, a few convicted, and the rest challenged. When it was over and I had time to reflect, I became emotionally overwhelmed, which was all quite strange to me since I'm not an emotional person; however, I became aware of how humbling the experience proved to be. God had powerfully used me after I had so terribly failed Him. He had revealed in a simple way what I had missed by running my own race in my own strength.

It was then I realized that it was God's work, God's calling, and God's plan being done God's way. I had done all past religious activities in my own power according to my own logic, based on what I thought my calling was in order to bring forth a vague notion of God's plan, and it always fell flat. There was no impact, no real change, no lives touched or challenged. At best I tested people's patience because of my zealous, immature, carnal ways or I made them angry, but there was clearly no authority or power behind what I had done.

I found myself at a crossroad. Did I want to settle for my best or learn to wait upon the Lord to lead me to His best? To me there was no real choice. I had already decided I would never turn back, and I needed to follow the Lord Jesus wherever He led me. It was clear I still had much to learn, but I had come too far, experienced too much, and knew what inner satisfaction and peace felt like to ever go back to one dead end after another, to taste of endless, lifeless activities that left me frustrated, and ultimately coming face-to-face with the emptiness of it all.

I was meditating on all of the events that happened as I came back to my table only to discover someone else was in my place. I was confused and I looked around and noticed an empty chair that was closer to the Lord. As I stood there trying to understand what was going on, I saw the Lord smile and point at the empty chair as if to say, "This is your chair, come and sit."

The Seeking Heart

New love seems simple enough, but when challenged, infant love will falter. The Shulamite girl knew she belonged to her beloved and that he belonged to her, but her love for him had not been firmly established. She was not fully prepared to commit all to him. It is not that the problem rested with him, but within her. There were flaws in her own character that wanted to cling to past selfish sentiment and pleasurable experiences.

Her past experiences with him at the banqueting table had brought sweet affections to her heart but now he was asking her to step outside of her comfort zones of what brought incredible personal security and pleasure to her and follow him into unknown territories. She wanted to hold onto to the sentiment, while controlling her present encounters with him by somehow recapturing those wonderful feelings that made her time with him so special, but deep in her heart she knew that such times were now in the past.

She first wanted the daybreak to cause the shadows of confusion to flee, and until then she would ask him to depart from her until she could make sense out of the confusing mess and situate the circumstances that would revive the former feelings and set up the right environment to continue where they left off.

Love was simple, but she didn't realize she had just complicated it by putting it into an emotional arena that desired to experience only that which would bring her pleasure. The desire to control her experience with him was causing the shadow of confusion to descend on her. He wanted to lead her into a deeper relationship with him, but she was content to hold onto the sentiment. He wanted a new day to dawn upon their love and she wanted to hold onto the fading glory of love that would eventually die on the vine if it didn't come to an abiding place where a more substantial union was clearly established with her beloved.

She assumed that she knew where to find him. He would be feeding among the lilies, but she failed to recognize that the mountain of "Bether" represented separation.[37] When a shepherd desires to lead his sheep to higher places, but they insist on remaining in a place that will become stagnant and cause the spirit to wither, it will cause a separation. A good shepherd will not drive his sheep, rather he calls them to follow him to new pastures. The Shulamite girl heard the call but would not follow, and as a result a separation had definitely occurred between them. She assumed that when she was ready, she could go to him among the lilies, or that he would possibly see her reasoning and come back to her to somehow fit into the reality she so desired.

The Shulamite girl realized in the night her grave error.[38] She actually was desiring the feeling itself more than her beloved. The whole situation showed her, her own immaturity in the relationship. After all, there is no greater sign of immaturity than the degree of selfishness that is reigning, and her selfishness was center stage. How could she make her love towards him fickle and worthless and his so cheap by not valuing him? How foolish she had been!

Who would have thought that the night would reveal the darkness in her own character? The silence of the darkness not only illuminated her character but it brought desperation with it. She had to find her beloved because she realized how much she loved him. She recognized that since she asked him to depart that she was the one who would have to step outside of her comfort zone and truly seek him.

She rose out of her bed. How ironic the whole scene became to her. He had invited her to rise up and follow him, but she had failed to do so, and now in the dark of the night she rises up to seek him in the streets

---

[37] Song of Solomon 2:16-17
[38] Song of Solomon 3:1

and broad ways of the city. She had no idea as to where he was and even asked the watchmen if they had seen him.[39]

It is hard to find someone we have sent away or let go of because of foolish notions. We often find ourselves seeking such individuals in darkness because we are at a loss as to where they can be found, and the dark night of our soul does not have the ability to illuminate that which is lost. The watchmen couldn't help because they weren't seeking him; therefore, they were not watching for him.

The girl was becoming more desperate to find her beloved. As she passed beyond the watchmen, to her relief her beloved allowed himself to be found by her. She had learned her lesson and now she clung to him, vowing to never let him depart from her again. This time she took him beyond the wall that had initially hid him, and the lattice that had concealed him from her, beyond the shuttered windows right into the chamber she had been conceived in to commune with him.[40]

It was a blessed time of communion that was enfolded with sweetness filling the air, as joy took flight on the wings of blessed grace, and rest settled on her soul. Once again, the girl charges the young handmaidens to not disrupt her beloved and their blessed time together.[41]

The Desperate Soul
(The Second Companion)

In the night the guilt and shame that had made their appearance at twilight were now mocking the former slave tenaciously. She had failed to respond to her redeemer, her Lord. Granted, she was chosen, but she was being prepared to take his side in service to those who belonged to his estate and kingdom. She was now finding herself to be a miserable slave because she refused to totally consecrate herself to him as a bondservant. Slaves were destined to serve, but they could

---

[39] Song of Solomon 3:2-3
[40] Song of Solomon 3:4; Jeremiah 29:13
[41] Song of Solomon 3:5

determine the quality of their service whether it was surface, half-hearted, or whether they completely sold out to serve their master the rest of their life. She didn't know what was stopping her from totally consecrating herself, but it was obvious that she was still holding onto some fear or right.[42]

The clear example of His leadership to her since she had been sitting at his table had revealed that he was foremostly a servant to his people. As she considered his latest call to her, it was that of a shepherd whose desire was to lead her to refreshing waters and pastures that would quiet her inner struggle, enabling her to grow and establish a sure footing in their relationship, but she failed to discern his call or understand his intentions towards her.[43] She realized that she had simply failed to trust his character even though he had proven trustworthy, and such failure revealed she was not prepared to follow him into the unknown.

Clearly, her suspicion towards his intentions had caused her logic to stand up in the courtroom of reason to make sense of his timing and his purpose without first considering who he had proven to be to her time and again. As king he ruled his kingdom with benevolence, as lord he ruled his household with grace and kindness, and as redeemer he had made it clear that he purchased her to not simply serve him, but serve with him in a place of royalty.

Her failure to trust him had caused her to recoil backwards into a morbid state. He didn't deserve such a response from her. It was clear that her inaction revealed that she was not even a dutiful servant that adhered to his requests.[44] She understood she was there in preparation to serve, but her position at his table and her undefined responsibility as a servant had collided, leaving her in a state of confusion and despair.

What was her real place? At first, she thought she understood her place, but her Lord's example of humble servitude as king caused her to rethink what her duty looked like. If she understood her place, she would be more prepared to respond. If she understood her duties, she

---

[42] Deuteronomy 15:12-17
[43] Psalm 23:1-4: Jeremiah 29:11
[44] Luke 6:46

would be clear as to her place, but it seemed that both aspects were uncertain and created a grey area instead of bringing clarity.

As she wrestled with her questions, a small light began to penetrate her understanding. As it parted the grey area, a simple picture emerged causing awe to rise up in her soul. And, what did the picture reveal? She realized her place was not determined by her position or her duties, but by her relationship with her Lord.

She chided herself. How could she have missed such a simple truth? Here she sat at her Lord's table trying to figure out her place so she could carry out her responsibility, while all the time she was where she needed to be. It was obvious that her Lord was not interested in some mechanical response on her part. He wanted her responses to come from a heart of love and as her love developed and changed for him, her place and responsibility would become clear.

She had so enjoyed sitting at the table with him, but had failed to advance her love for him by following him into the next stage of their relationship in order to be prepared to take her rightful place. Suddenly, an overwhelming desperation flooded her soul. She had to find him and tell him what she realized and ask him to forgive her for her foolishness and assure him that she had learned her lesson: that it was never really about her place and responsibility; rather, it was about their relationship.

She realized that his heart was to always have a relationship with her, but she had been trying to make sure that she kept her place at his table instead of establishing a place in her heart for her love to grow for him. Clearly, it was not his love that made her unsure; rather, it was her faltering love that caused her to transpose her insecurities onto him. If he was to entrust her with the important matters of his heart, he had to know that her heart was steadfast towards him, faithful, and pure.[45]

As she stood at the door, looking into the night, she was faced with the fact that she had no idea where he could be. It was clear that her desperation would not let her off the hook, nor would her guilt simply let her stand in the doorway, or her tormenting shame let her hide any longer. She had to do something to find him and set the record straight.

---

[45] Psalm 16:8

She found herself fleeing into the darkness, looking for someone who might point her to him. Perhaps those who guarded the entrances of his kingdom would surely know where he was, but when she sought them out, they could only shrug their shoulders. Maybe those who attended His sheep could tell her where he was, but when asked, they admitted they had been with the sheep and not the shepherd.

Her desperation grew as those she encountered along the way couldn't help her, but she was resolved to search until she found him.[46] She had hoped that someone could point her in the right direction, but it was then that she recognized the immaturity of her love. She would have known where to find Him if she had a better relationship with him. He knew all about her, but she didn't really know him. She sat at his table, but she never walked with him in the night. She shared bits of her heart, but he didn't share his thoughts. She had been so needy that their times together had been taken up with her. In her immaturity, it was clear she had been silly towards him and foolish about real love.

As she faced her foolishness, it was as if she came to the end of herself with nowhere to go, and it was then that she became aware of a garden. She remembered he had mentioned working in a run-down garden that had much potential but needed a great deal of attention to make it a desirable place of fellowship. It dawned on her the garden he was talking about was to be a place of fellowship for them.

She also suddenly realized that she knew where that garden was located. It was tucked away from the rest of the world, and she had a clear sense that it was right in front of her. She also suspected he was waiting for her to take the initiative to seek him out with her heart, and in doing so, he would be found by her.

Find him, she did. It was as though he had been waiting for her to remember what he had told her. She fell before him and clung to him, crying and confessing the indifference of her heart towards him and the error of her ways. He gently raised her up and smiled at her.

She knew that all was well between them, and this time she was the one who took his hand and led him back to the place of sweet fellowship.

---

[46] Jeremiah 29:13

She was almost giddy in her joy as they walked together in the coolness of the night.

It was clear she had crossed an important threshold in their relationship. She had learned an important lesson about love. Love is what defines not only the quality and type of relationship that is established, but also the place one is to take in that union, as well as the responsibility one is to assume in it to ensure love's integrity.

Growing

Love

The Disciplines
of the Cross

What does it mean for love to grow? Clearly, the love I speak of is not the love of the world which is nothing more than lust that is propped up by selfishness, swinging from fanciful limbs of expectation with no place to comfortably land when it comes to reality. Such love has no substance, no foundation, and no room to take root and mature.

Godly love comes only from God and is experienced in times of sweet fellowship. It finds its authority and strength in the moral obligation to do right by those it is directed at. It takes responsibility for its attitude and conduct towards others. Its greatest quality is that it is selfless. It will submit to that which is worthy for the benefit of others, as it is always looking for ways to honor and serve others that encourages, inspires, and brings freedom so they can reach the heights of their potential. And, how do I know this? "For God so loved the world, that he gave his only begotten Son, that whosoever believeth in him should not perish, but have everlasting life" (John 3:16).

We all start out with our personal ideas of love. These ideas come from the world's propaganda machine that can be encouraged, translated, or adjusted to fit the environment that is most affecting us, whether it be family, friends or peers. When I first encountered the love of God at salvation, I was overwhelmed, but I still operated from my own fanciful concepts of love in my early years as a Christian.

Natural love will easily set you up to work in a fleshy, sentimental sphere where lusts motivate, pride seeks a place to supremely rule, and fickle feelings determine the level of commitment. I learned from personal experiences that such a premise will let you down because it is surface, conditional, oppressive, touchy, and self-serving. However, the failure of fickle love in my life caused me to press more into the Lord to bring perspective to His love. I found myself in the inner chambers, ever seeking His viewpoint. Every new discovery made me realize what a spiritual wilderness I had been in because so much of what I understood about relationships, commitments, and love was still very much based on self-serving notions and the world.

At the table of Jesus, He ceased to be in the shadows of my understanding or on the perimeters of vague notions. I was beginning to chew on the deeper realities of God. I began to see God's love from a heavenly perspective that became overpowering to me to such an extent that my attitude was being transformed and my definition of it was being redefined. I was being led out of my personal barren wilderness of ignorance, brought on by worldly influences, that had often caused me to slip into a confusing state where I became lost in the vain, senselessness of something that had no real substance, that were clearly tainted and based on notions that were not realistic.

Sitting at Jesus' table proved to be an incredible, life-changing experience for me. Learning of Him caused my appreciation and love to grow for Him. He ceased to be shrouded in sentiment or fanciful expectation as I became more aware of what was important to Him by discovering His attitudes about different matters and the intent behind His teachings.

As I learned about Jesus, I began to understand who I was in Christ. My identity had been based on illusive religious concepts, but as I became more cognizant of who Jesus was, my life began to be redefined. The reality of Galatians 2:20 became vibrant as I realized that the Apostle Paul was simply defining the Christian life as living the life of Christ by faith and not according to one's own ideas of life.

I was excited about imparting the truths that were taking root in my soul to others. However, I was beginning to learn that ministry is about timing—God's timing, and that all my ideas, agendas, and notions had to be out of the way before the Lord used me. If I felt self-sufficient towards a matter or had strong feelings about it, He would not call me to do the task even though He had assigned it to me.[1] Thus, the task simply laid before me, undone and pending, ever challenging me.

---

[1] 2 Corinthians 3:5

There were so many times I wanted to run with the task before me but I couldn't because the Lord had not given me marching orders. I tried to calm my tendencies to figure out some plan on my own, as well as pull back my emotional momentum to push ahead of Him before receiving the appropriate nod that gave me the go ahead.

Another aspect I was learning about ministry at Jesus' table entailed stepping out by faith and availing myself to share at different times. For example, I would feel an impression to ask certain people in leadership positions to speak at the church I attended. One pastor allowed it, while an elder who was filling in at the pulpit until a pastor could be chosen, ignored it. When the door was closed in my face, I would ask the Lord if I was hearing from Him, or was I simply being impulsive. After encountering a mixture of open and closed doors, the Lord revealed to me that the test was not about open or closed doors but availability and faithfulness. It didn't matter whether a door opened or closed because He is the one who controls the doors of opportunities. My obligation was simple and always remained the same, to be faithful to knock on such doors, while trusting Him to open the ones He has ordained, and then be faithful to take hold of such openings in obedience before the door slammed shut.[2]

Through each experience of the open door of opportunity, I soon learned that all ministry had to be about Him, and had to be void of any personal interest or carried out in personal strength to avoid the temptation that comes with spiritual accomplishments and victories: that of touching His glory by taking personal credit for His work.[3] I quickly learned that the presence of any emotional momentum and personal strengths had to first recede into an attitude of reluctance in carrying out such tasks, before I was able to carry it out in the right spirit of humility. It became obvious that the more self was out of the way the greater the opportunity for the Lord to do a great and lasting work in people's lives.

It was becoming clear to me that I had been a Mary, sitting at Jesus' feet as others served at the table.[4] I was being prepared to serve, but I

---

[2] Luke 16:10; Revelation 3:7
[3] 1 Corinthians 1:31
[4] Luke 10:38-42

didn't know in what capacity. My few years at the table taught me to wait on the Lord, and to know that before He would entrust me with the affairs of His kingdom, I first had to discern my motives and my intents to make sure I was out of the way.

I knew I was being prepared at His table to actually respond to His voice. He would simply smile and nod a certain direction when it came to ministry, while the Holy Spirit would take the truths of the Word and impart them to me, filling me up daily, preparing me to walk them out in the mundane activities of life. I didn't realize while sitting at the table that my ears were being finetuned to hear what the Spirit was saying. After all, He is the one who only speaks what He hears from the throne as He leads believers into all truth about Jesus.[5]

Unbeknown to me the call I would hear next wouldn't be to serve, but that of being His disciple. I really thought since I had been prepared at the table that it would be for service, but in reality, I was being prepared to carry a cross. This cross would help me to learn what it meant to follow Jesus.[6]

True discipleship will naturally bring you back to the work of Christ. All matters must begin with His redemption, line up to His righteousness before it can end with a greater revelation of Him. I would learn there are different sides to the cross, the back, the sides, and the front.

It's not unusual for some people when they first come to the cross of Christ to stand in its shadows, whether it is behind the cross or to the side as they consider how they will respond to it, while others seek the light of the cross to deal with their sins. Shadows allow some to keep their dignity intact to avoid the harsh reality of their sin, while maintaining some type of distance where they can glance at the cross to avoid becoming too involved with its real work of consecration. However, there are those who seek the light of it, knowing it will not only expose their sin but bring cleansing to the soul.

I initially sought the light of the cross because I had no doubt about my sins, but I failed to realize that to enjoy the full work of redemption, I had to become identified with His cross. It was not just a matter of

---

[5] John 16:13
[6] Luke 9:23-25

standing or kneeling in front of it seeking forgiveness, but it was also a matter of entering into the death of the self-life to ensure the old ways are put in the grave in order to be raised up in the newness of Christ's life, thereby, taking on His likeness and reflecting His glory.[7]

I had read the likes of Matthew 16:24-26, where Jesus was calling His disciples to take up the cross to follow Him, as well as Romans 6:3-14 that talks about complete identification with the work of Jesus' cross, but I had failed to completely embrace His cross to become identified to His work and His life. I had initially enjoyed the light of the cross and was greatly attracted to its challenge, but I ended up walking into the shadows of the cross to serve Him according to my misconceived notions, which prevented the deeper work of His cross to be accomplished in my life.

I had tried to define my own idea of Christianity while falling prey to circumstances that often ended up defining my attitude and actions as unfruitful. In a sense, I had become a cork on the ocean of life tossed to and fro by situations because I was not grounded on the Rock or fully connected to the Vine.[8] I had often groped in the darkness of my own understanding, while walking in circles and ending up at the same dead ends that marked my failures with a sense of hopelessness.

Although I had denied myself here and there to obey the tasks set before me at His table, I was about to learn what denying self really entailed. We can somewhat think it quite honorable to bear a cross. It points to the idea of suffering for great causes, but when the prerequisite to carrying the cross is denying self, it strips away such prideful notions. It took a while for me to discover that if denial does not occur first, the pride of the self-life becomes an arrogant martyr that seeks recognition for its "supposedly" great sacrifice.

As the Lord began to show me my pride, I began to understand what I had to deny. "Deny" points to "disowning" self. This means denying self of its rights to life on its terms. On the throne of the self-life sits the pride of life, and pride is the epitome of selfishness, whether it is self-absorbed, self-centered, or self-serving. As the great idol of humanity, it

---

[7] Psalm 17:15; Romans 6:3-6; 8:29; 2 Corinthians 3:18
[8] John 15:1-8; 1 Corinthians 3:11; Ephesians 4:14

demands worship, adherence, and obedience. It wants to call the shots as it sees itself deserving of special recognition. It plays on emotions to manipulate, feeds egos to come out on top, intimidates to control, and is ruthless in getting what it wants. It is the tyrant in its kingdom, a moral despot in its pursuits, a traitor to those who dare trust it, a cruel executor to those who challenge it, and will always set people up to fall into mockery, disparity, and destruction. It wants all the glory even though it tries to nobly humble itself in the sight of others, but it always does so with the intent of being lifted up in some type of exaltation. Pride is so many things, except genuine love.

Pride has no room for genuine love. It must survive at all costs; therefore, it knows nothing of sacrifice. It must always be honored; therefore, it cannot afford to prefer others over itself without ultimately being honored in the end. It is committed to getting its way and proves to be conditional in its love and kind acts; therefore, it knows nothing of real selfless commitment.

The Lord first took a spoon to my pride. I realized later that He was exposing the very tip of it. It caused a bit of discomfort, but I didn't understand how pride invades every area of one's life. It can be a look (smug), a feeling (self-sufficient), an attitude (haughty/judgmental), a way of thinking (conceit), a way of walking (arrogance, anger), and a way of holding self in an unyielding manner (stiff-necked).

Next, He took a shovel to my pride causing embarrassment. Embarrassment simply means your pride has been offended, making you feel foolish about something. Such an affront to your pride has a way of making an impression on you that will not be quickly forgotten. The other part of this embarrassment is that you realize that you have embarrassed yourself many times before without recognizing it.

This is when you grasp the shocking reality of how your pride has blinded you to yourself. It is the board in the eye that allows you to see the faults of everyone else, but it keeps you from seeing the flaws of your character, the error of your ways, and the unacceptable fruit your life is producing.[9]

---

[9] Matthew 7:1-5

It was hard to look into the face of my insidious pride. It was clear that I wanted to avoid such embarrassment, but having your pride offended is not the same thing as overcoming it. Pride is at the base of the "old man" and it must be completely exposed to strip it of its reign, which brings me to the final measure the Lord used on my pride. He used a backhoe, and He went deep, into the very basement to expose every insidious way in which it operates.

Oh! how He worked that backhoe! Deeper and deeper He went, unearthing the stench of my pride. I was overwhelmed with repulsion, embarrassment, and fell in utter despair by what He uncovered. It seemed that every shovelful of my pride left me feeling more uncertain as to who I was in the scheme of things. I finally said, "Lord, if you go any deeper, there will be nothing left of me."

I will never forget His reply, "That's the idea."

Royalty After All

The Shulamite girl had spent precious time with her beloved in her mother's chamber. He had first come to her as king to invite her to His table and feast under a banner of love. After a time of separation, He came to her as a shepherd to lead her into a deeper relationship with him, but she failed to respond. Her failure to follow had caused him to depart, compelling her in the night to rise up in desperation to find him.

When she found him, she clung to him and led him into the secret chamber of her conception to become more established in their love. She had realized how her love faltered and failed to respond to his invitation, causing a temporary separation that she wanted to prevent at any cost.

Their time in the chamber was precious. She came out cherishing their love and valuing him, but she knew that there was more to love. No doubt her love for him had been clearly established and she had found rest in his love, but now it had to grow. She had wandered in the spiritual wilderness long enough because of silly notions, and now it was time for her to not only mature in her understanding of love, but to allow it to cause her to grow into it as a woman.

She realized that for people to grow in love they first have to let go of their foolish ideas, allowing love to mature in regard to how they will respond and handle it. Clearly, in new love there is no deep commitment and in faltering love there is no enduring character. A deep commitment comes out of faithfulness that proves to be steadfast, while enduring character comes out of testing.

As the Shulamite girl pondered the possibilities, she noticed her beloved coming out of the wilderness.[10] He was emerging out of the shadows of her understanding to once again reveal himself to her, but this time he was coming to her as king. It was then that she understood that love grows when authority and position is properly established. It is one thing to be a lamb being cared for by the committed shepherd and another matter altogether when it comes to a king coming to his beloved, dressed in his royal apparel and surrounded by his valiant soldiers.

It was obvious that at this point it was not a matter of following her beloved but being prepared in his presence to take her rightful position. People never grow in integrity unless they are challenged, and the only way for a person to be effectively challenged is for his or her position to be revealed so the individual can actually grow into it. For her, she was to grow into the position of royalty. However, to reach her potential in her royal position would require inward disciplines.

True love can only grow in the arena of disciplines. Love to fickle flesh is like the dross intermingled with gold that must be brought to the top and skimmed in order to ensure its purity. Therefore, any love associated with the flesh must be reduced into a puddle of desperation to be skimmed off before it can come forth as pure, enduring, and sacrificial. It is only as authority and responsibility are established in light of position can a person become a true follower of the shepherd into a life of acceptable service.

As she considered the pillars of smoke announcing the advancement of her beloved king, she was reminded of Mount Sinai smoking in the midst of thundering and lightnings and the noise of the trumpet, along with the cloudy pillar that descended and stood at the door of the tabernacle so that Yahweh could talk to His servant, Moses.

---

[10] Song of Solomon 3:6

91

It was also a pillar that Jacob had erected and anointed before Yahweh to memorialize his meeting with his Creator and the vow he made with Him.[11] The Shulamite girl knew the smoke represented holiness and that the purging fire was often shrouded by it, while the perfume not only represented a fragrance made fit for Yahweh, but it pointed to that which was anointed and would prove to be attractive to all who encountered the king along the way.

She had to ponder what her king was riding on. It was not a horse pulling a chariot, but his bed.[12] It was clear that he did not fear an attack for his work was done and he was at peace. His valiant men were on guard ready to do battle in his stead, but she also realized the nighttime that would cover enemy attack was not yet upon them. Instead of coming in preparation for some engagement or unpleasant encounter, he was at rest, ready to commune with those who found their place with him.

The Shulamite girl could see that the king's particular chariot was made with the preferred wood of Lebanon. It was such a strong wood that it withstood and grew straight and tall in spite of the elements. Wood often represents humanity, but it is the reality of Yahweh in the midst of mankind that is the true source of strength. The pillars of silver point to redemption. It reminded her that her people were purchased by Yahweh and that she belonged to the eternal King of heaven. The chariot was surrounded with gold that spoke of Israel's divine calling, and the color of purple which pointed to royalty.[13]

It was during this time that the daughters of Zion were commanded to go forth to prepare and declare that the one who was designated by his mother as being set apart as king, was now coming to claim the ones who had been promised to him.[14] Such an occasion would be a time of expectation and rejoicing.

However, as the king came forth, he once again set his eyes upon her and the words that followed caused wonderment to her soul which

---

[11] Genesis 28:11-19; Exodus 19:16-20:19; 33:9
[12] Song of Solomon 3:7,8
[13] Song of Solomon 3:9,10
[14] Song of Solomon 3:11

settled into quiet confidence that he recognized that her love for him had indeed grown. The first word "Behold" required one to know who or what he was seeing.[15] It was clear that the king wanted others to see in her what he was seeing.

His initial description of her was like the others before. She was his fair one who was pleasant to look upon. However, his description of her eyes being that of a dove revealed that she had developed purity in becoming single in her focus towards him. She knew that her eyes were highlighted by her hair, but what followed revealed that her present love for him was far out-weighing the faltering love that had been left outside the door of her mother's chambers.[16]

The king said her hair was like the flock of goats that appeared at Mount Gilead. Goats held a significant place in Jewish religious practices. Dark goat's hides were used as a covering in the second layer of the tabernacle pointing to sin. The Shulamite girl understood that the second layer of goat skins were over the most beautiful layer of the tabernacle that spoke of heaven (blue), royalty (purple), and sacrifice (scarlet), and the goat skins were covered by the third layer of dyed red ram's skins that pointed to atonement that God provided through sacrifices to cover the sins of Israel. The fourth and outer layer was the badger skins. They were brown and blended in with the countryside.[17] Goats were also used on the Day of Atonement. One goat was used as a sin offering, while the other became a scapegoat that was sent off in the wilderness with all the sins of Israel for the year.[18]

Like the badger skin that blended into the countryside, man who was formed from the dust of the earth, also blends in with the barren terrain of the world, reminding him that, at best, he will only leave behind the fading footprints of humanity. It was also clear that man's sins needed to be atoned for, but what is most important is what is inside of man.

---

[15] Song of Solomon 4:1
[16] Ibid
[17] Exodus 26:1, 14. The representation of the different materials used in the construction of the tabernacle can be found in various books written on this subject, but the source I use the most is, "The Dwelling Place for God," by Ruth Specter Lascelle, © 1990 by Hyman Israel Specter.
[18] Song of Solomon 4:1; Leviticus 16:5-22

Man has to be marked by a heavenly identity, illuminated by royalty, and sealed with forgiveness to possess hope and know satisfaction.

The location of these goats was important as well. Gilead was a place of abundance where the goats would be satisfied. It was a place of healing, for out of Gilead came healing balm that was valued.[19] The Shulamite girl began to recognized how love had brought healing and satisfaction to her soul, marking growth, not only in her relationship with her beloved but in her personal character.

The hair of the goat was long. Uncut hair for a man often identified him as being a Nazarite who was identified to a vow of consecration. The covering of the hair pointed to the man submitting himself to this vow. The great judge, Samson toyed with sin and found himself in a compromising position and lost his strength when his hair was cut. As for the woman, she automatically had the covering of submission due to her hair, but whether she came into such submission in the appropriate way depended on whether her heart was humble and tender before Yahweh.[20]

The mention of her teeth made her smile.[21] The condition of the teeth determined the health of a creature, and she was aware that her teeth were straight, and were being highlighted by her smile. It was clear that her beloved was not only noting the health of their love, but he was acknowledging that she was now assimilating the affairs of their relationship in a proper way. Her past notions about love were silly and her previous advancement in love lacked substance, but there was a strength in her present love that had been shaped and developed by experience.

The fact that he also noted a flock of sheep reminded her that before Moses led the children of Israel to the Promised Land and David was king, they were both shepherds. These two great leaders never lost the shepherd's heart towards Israel, but Israel was not always prepared to follow their godly shepherds. They often proved to be like the wool. The wool of the sheep was used to clothe the outer body of man but only the

---

[19] Jeremiah 8:22, 46:11; 50:19; Micah 7:14
[20] Numbers 6:1-9; Judges 16:16-22 1 Corinthians 11:15
[21] Song of Solomon 4:2

linens covered the priest, and the nation of Israel was called to be a royal priesthood. [22] The wool represented the carnal man still bound to earth, while the linen pointed to righteousness that marked a spiritual, heavenly man who was consecrated to stand between earth and heaven. It was clear the transition from goats to sheep pointed to the fact that much of her independence had given way to submission where she now had the liberty to follow her beloved as a shepherd.

She was awed when her beloved mentioned her lips were like a thread of scarlet and her speech comely. One of the women she admired was Rahab. She was a woman of vision, faith, and courage and as a result she was given a promise. A thread of scarlet identified her and her household to that promise—that they would be spared from the judgment that came upon Jericho. She became the great-grandmother of King David. The Shulamite girl's beloved was associating her as being such a woman of courage and faith, identifying her to redemption and a promise.[23]

In the past her speech had lacked temperance and wisdom. In a sense he was saying that her lips were not only an expression of redemption and great promise, but they had been purged in such a way that her speech had ceased to be that of a silly young inexperienced girl. Her words now pointed to wisdom and discretion that possessed authority.

The mention of her temples or cheeks in regard to the pomegranate brought such delight to her soul.[24] Her cheeks were covered by her hair and she was beginning to understand that it is true that so much of love finds it source in chambers of communion. Only her beloved could understand and appreciate it, while the rest of the world could never know of it. However, real love produces fruits, and it was clear her love for the king was producing fruit sweet to him, but the pomegranate had many seeds that had great potential to multiply and produce tasty red fruit. This fruit would reveal the quality of itself as soon as it was opened, allowing others to partake of it.

---

[22] Exodus 3:1; 39:27,28 1 Samuel 16:11-13
[23] Joshua 2:17,18; 6:17; Song of Solomon 4:3
[24] Song of Solomon 4:3

The Shulamite girl realized that real love is meant to multiply. Granted, it is established in sweet places of communion, but it is meant to be shared. Once such love is allowed to touch others, they likewise will know the quality of its sweetness. It was becoming clear that it was time to allow her love for the king to multiply itself in other ways to ensure greater growth.

As the king mentioned the shape of her neck, she realized that her love was no longer dangling according to her fickle self-will, but was now clearly established in that which was eternal, steadfast, and fortified by Yahweh.[25] He was now the source of her love because He had erected such love in the midst of His people, giving them the opportunity to find strength and comfort in it. It was clear that her love was now becoming prized by her beloved, because it was not just greatly valued, but its preciousness was well guarded and protected.

Her love was now mature enough to avoid landing on personal strength, but to also seek the strength of her beloved's love as well. It became clear that her love had graduated from him simply resting between child-like faith and grace in her heart to her becoming like a young antelope that now not only stood, but ran to places where she could partake of and enjoy the bounty of their love together.[26] After all, love was not just a place of abiding fellowship, but it served as the inspiration to walk in faith, seek mercy and strength in times of failure and need, to receive grace with an open heart, and rest in assurance of its abiding protection.

Now that her love for her beloved enabled her to stand in assurance and walk by faith, she could now follow him whenever he called her. She had learned that she could not seek him until the light broke on the terrain before her, but it had become clear to her that it was time for her to rise up and seek after him to acquire a deeper fellowship.[27] She recognized that he had come to her before and met her in her state, but now it was time for her to seek him in higher places that would cause

---

[25] Song of Solomon 4:4
[26] Song of Solomon 4:5
[27] Song of Solomon 4:6

their love to become a sweet savor brought forth by death to what was, in order to produce the heavenly fragrance of what could be.[28]

Clearly, her love for him had taken root, but now it must take hold, and the only way it could take hold was by her becoming identified with her beloved in every aspect of his life. She realized in her immature love, his love for her had to be constantly compensated by him, by seeking her out and ever challenging her to rise up, but it was now time for her love to voluntarily reach up and take hold of a greater identification with him to ensure deeper fellowship.

As she was meditating on this, she heard him speak again, "Thou are all fair, my love; there is no spot in thee."[29] My, how far she had come because of his love! She started out dark, but at the present he couldn't find any spot in her. Because of his love she stood pure before him and now it was only right for her love to respond to him.

He spoke again, "Come with me from Lebanon, my spouse..."[30]

Letting Go
(The Second Companion)

Everyone has an idea of love, but the former slave realized she didn't know what constituted love. In her initial love, she felt an appreciation for her Lord rescuing her from the auction block, while in her faltering love she experienced the desperation of making sure the relationship was right after failing to respond to him, but past those two stages she was left in a quandary.

It's natural to think love is easy, but in reality, discovering what true love is requires a journey that takes one past self-interest to discover the interests of another. It was true that she had feelings for her Lord, but love is more than feelings. She clearly had an appreciation for what He did for her, but she had not developed an appreciation for who he was. She sensed if her feelings and appreciation did not graduate

---

[28] 2 Corinthians 2:15,16
[29] Song of Solomon 4:7
[30] Song of Solomon 4:8

beyond mere sentiment and a sense of indebtedness, they would morph into methodical reaction instead of a response of love.

She wanted to understand what love meant and how it manifested itself. She realized that her ideas of love were a product of her own unrealistic ideas that bowed before her, while exalting her in her mind to be a recipient of some type of silly adoration, while making her the center of all matters. In her Lord, she had seen real love in action. It was not self-centered, self-serving, and/or desirous of silly adoration.

It was true that at the table her Lord had initially put all the focus and emphasis on her, but she was becoming more aware that it was his way of serving as an inspiration of real love to her and as an example of how it serves others. His love was to inspire her to love him, while his visible example of love was to show her how to honor him by loving, caring for, and serving others.[31]

Once again, she realized that she was more concerned about figuring out how she could keep her position at his table rather than learning of him so she would know how to serve him. Before he had redeemed her, she served to survive the cruelty of her master, but now she would have to learn what it would mean to serve out of genuine love.

At the table she was learning the obvious things about him. He was, in a sense, teaching her what was important to the matters of his household and preparing her to follow him into a life of true service in his kingdom, but she had been missing the real purpose of their time together. She had been trying to learn what to do, while failing to learn to discern those matters that would reveal more of her Lord's heart and character so she could truly please him. She was starting to realize it was not about her doing something right to keep her master at bay, but getting him right as to his person and way of doing things in order to bring him closer to her heart.

She had to acknowledge that her perception of him was based on her heart attitude towards life in general.[32] It was clear that her heart attitude had been slowly changing, allowing the shadows of her own

---

[31] John 3:16; 1 John 4:19
[32] Proverbs 4:23

insecurities to part so that she could see him more clearly, but there were still areas of grey.

At first, she had been hard towards him because her heart was cold and she didn't trust anyone. As she began to realize he was sincere, she considered him through stones and rocks of skepticism and speculation that only would allow her to let him in so far. It was always clear to her that she was ready at all times to put those rocks up as a wall against him if he made a move that created fear in her.[33]

As she became more comfortable with her household position and duties, she took more time and pleasure in them, which translated into failure on her part to seek out time with her Lord. This caused what she had learned at the table to recede back into some storage area of her mind, where dust often collected, covering over what had been initially prized by her.[34]

It was slowly dawning on her that real love was a matter of the heart. When present, it inspired those with open hearts to cast aside fleshly, fickle love to reach the heights of its excellent ways. It was true her Lord's love had inspired her at times, but fear and procrastination tripped her up, revealing that she was in many ways still half-hearted towards aspects of her life with him.[35]

It was becoming obvious that she had to be willing to give her whole heart to her Lord if she was going to develop the type of life and disciplines that would ensure the integrity of her relationship with him, and her service with him.

She chided herself as she realized that many times when there was some lapse in her fellowship with him that she had easily forgotten what he had done for her—how he had rescued her from the auction block and brought her into his kingdom to sit at his dinner table. [36]

He made sure she was clothed with the best to distinguish her place. She wore the finest gold and gems to highlight that she was part of

---

[33] Matthew 13:4-6, 18-21
[34] Matthew 13:7, 22
[35] 1 John 4:18,19
[36] 2 Peter 1:9,10

royalty. She had been graced with beauty even though inwardly she occasionally struggled with the ugliness of her past.[37]

It was also true that all was made available at the table for her to partake of, but initially she suffered from malnutrition and lacked the appetite for the foods that graced his table. He had been so patient with her to give her milk and a bit a bread while she slowly gained an appetite for foods that possessed sustenance and would ensure inner development and maturity. She not only had to gain a taste for such foods, but she had to learn to chew them in such a way that she could assimilate them.[38]

She realized that her time with him were times in which inner disciplines were being established and reinforced in her. As she examined where she had been and where she was, it became clear that even though she failed to understand what her ultimate goal should have been, she now possessed an inner beauty. She sighed because she knew he had brought that beauty out in her, but what did she bring out in him?

He was willing to pay all to redeem her, but she reserved the right to decide how far she would let him in, in what way she would serve him, and where she would follow him. He committed all for and to her, but she had been too self-absorbed to recognize it, and kept waiting for him to prove himself in unrealistic ways before offering her whole heart.

It was then that she realized she offered him nothing, and what she could offer him such as her life, heart, and real commitment, she had selfishly reserved for herself. She was looking for someone who could earn her love based on unobtainable, silly notions, while missing the essence of love that was right in front of her. It was then that she also began to understand that true love is not earned; rather, it is offered to whosoever will receive it. It is meant to be given away and not held in any personal reserves.

The former slave girl realized that she was no longer a slave girl enslaved to her past. His love had set her free to discover her beauty and now it was time for her to reach her potential. It was obvious her

---

[37] Isaiah 61:10
[38] John 4:34 compare with Romans 12:1,2; 1 Corinthians 3:1-3; Hebrews 5:12-14

Lord cherished her and now she must rise to the same excellent heights by cherishing him in the same way. She needed to match his commitment to take her place beside him. She would have to trust him with her whole heart with the same care and kindness he had given his heart to her if she was going to do right by him. She had to cast aside any personal rights or notions if she was going to follow him.[39]

It was clear as to what she needed to do. She needed to let go of the past and cast aside personal rights, and the next time he called her, there would be no hesitation on her part. She would rise up and follow him.

Identification

The walk of a disciple is not a glamorous walk. Sadly, many people have romanticized Jesus' cross by considering it in light of an honorable sacrifice. By glamorizing the cross of redemption, it is natural to embellish the idea of picking up a personal cross. The concept of dying for something noble is commendable and noteworthy; however, Paul made quite a statement in Romans 5:7, "For scarcely for a righteous man will one die: yet peradventure for a good man some would even dare to die."

The truth is we have a tendency to perceive that Jesus' death was commendable because He was dying for something worthy of such a sacrifice. After all, one who dies for something that is worthless would be considered a fool. The truth is Jesus died for mankind who is unworthy of any such consideration. When you realize that even after His great sacrifice many people would hate, rebel, and shake their fist at Him in rejection of the great work of His sacrifice, you again would have to question the reason God offered up such a sacrifice on our behalf, but then you suddenly realize it had nothing to do with man's worth, but with the harsh reality that only God could pay the acceptable debt for our sins and satisfy the just judgment that His holy Law required.

---

[39] Hebrews 12:1

Jesus' cross clearly revealed that He died on our behalf. In essence, He was dying for our sins because we couldn't pay the debt. However, our personal cross is not about dying **for** something; rather, it is about dying **to** something. This perspective takes any concept of nobility out of the picture when it comes to our personal cross.

When the Lord was dealing with my pride, it became more obvious to me that what the Bible said about my spiritual condition was correct. Intellectually, I chose to agree with God's Word, but it does not become a matter of truth until it is revealed to the heart by the Holy Spirit as being so.

The reality of my depravity was being brought front and center in light of my pride. Before I became a Christian, I was introduced to my spiritual plight by Romans 3:10, "There is none righteous, no not one." I clearly understood I had a sin problem. When I first became a Christian, I learned Isaiah 64:6, "But we are all as an unclean thing, and all our righteousnesses are as filthy rags; and we all do fade as a leaf; and our iniquities, like the wind, have taken us away." I realized all my past religious activities were unacceptable to the Lord and in fact, they were considered a stench, but what I failed to realize is that even as a Christian all deeds that originate from the flesh will be considered filthy rags before God. These deeds have no substance behind them and will be taken away by the winds of judgment along with personal strength.

As the Lord dealt with my pride, I was reminded of Romans 7:18, "For I know that in me (that is, in my flesh,) dwelleth no good thing; for to will is present with me; but how to perform that which is good I find not." It was my heart to do right, but my flesh often won out. Jesus said it best when He stated on the night of His betrayal that the spirit is willing but the flesh is weak.[40] I realized the only thing that could silence the power of the flesh in my life was the application of the cross to my old life.

As the Lord went deeper into my pride, these Scriptures all came together to form a mosaic of how far, how wide, and how extensive the corruption of my "old man" reached: it was complete. It penetrated every fiber of my being and I knew that it had become a wall against the

---

[40] Matthew 26:41

102

matters of God. God's love was selfless, but my pride was selfish. God's love was honorable, but my pride was self-serving, and I realized that the extent my pride reigned would determine the extent of my love for the Lord and acceptable service.

As the attitude and ways of the carnal man were being exposed, I became aware that the "old man" identified me to the base ways of the world and not to the excellent ways of heaven. The Lord was calling me higher, and before this revelation about my pride was revealed to me, I swung from the fragile limbs of worldly expectation and ended up colliding with some reality, which caused me to fall into a pit of despair. Once I climbed out of the pit, I relied on what I scripturally knew in order to work a matter out in my mind. Then I'd hit an immovable wall that left me feeling like a failure. I recognized that the carnal ways found their origins in the world and my pride.

The only way I could come higher was to daily deny my pride any audience, and allow the cross to go as deep as it could. Granted, it was bringing sorrow to my heart because each layer revealed my failure before the Lord. It caused depression to nip at my heels as I fought back the despair that there was nothing good in me that I could offer the Lord, and there was nothing I could do to change my identification to the world, except give way to the work of the cross.

The Apostle Paul spoke of being crucified to the world and the world crucified to him.[41] The flesh is the platform in which pride can sit on the throne of the self-life and the world can attract one's affection and take a person's lusts captive with its seduction and indoctrination. Nailing the "old man" to the cross not only crossed out pride's right to reign, as well as the influence and power of the "old man," it allowed one to become identified with Jesus in His cross. The more the "old man" is crucified, the more a person is lifted up by the work of the cross of Christ above the claims the world has on his or her soul.

This became obvious to me in my personal journey. The more I became identified with Jesus in His death, the more I found I was experiencing His life. Once I became identified in His burial, I realized that sin had no more claim on me because all my past sins were in the

[41] Galatians 6:14

grave.[42] Without the claim of sin upon my life, Satan had no case against me to present in the courts of heaven.

The real clincher came as I began to recognize the significance of Jesus' resurrection. The reality of sin will knock you off of the pinnacle of self-sufficiency, while the grave will bring you down to the foot of the cross and into empty chambers that represent the death and decay of everything associated with the condemned flesh, the carnal way, and the fading world.

It is vital we face the grave because that is where the ways of the "old man" will end. The flesh is clearly slated to die, the physical body to fall to the wayside, and the hold of earth upon us to let go. I found that as I allowed the cross to have its way, my attitude toward the world changed and my fleshly appetites began losing their power over me. The more the "old man" died, the greater my liberty to discover the heights of God.

It was as I let go that I was lifted up in newness of life to gain a greater perspective. There were so many times I was looking at the blowing trees of difficulty before me but couldn't see the forest. At such times a wrestling match would go on in my soul, and I found myself being enshrouded in darkness, but as I chose to trust the character of God instead of focusing on the circumstances, He would bring me to a place of spiritual rest.

Resting in Him allowed me to face the darkness with a quiet confidence. I remember reading a verse in Isaiah 30:15, "For thus saith the Lord GOD, the Holy One of Israel: In returning and rest shall ye be saved; in quietness and in confidence shall be your strength: and ye would not." There are those who want their way so badly that they will not give up the struggle in their soul and come to a place of faith so they can rest in what they know is true about the one true God.

The Lord was forever leading me to spiritual wildernesses, preparing me in darkness, whether it be in light of some loss, overwhelming challenges or through illnesses, ever testing my character, changing my direction, refining my calling, challenging my perception, and enlarging my faith. Every time the cross went deeper, it caused darkness in my

---

[42] Romans 6:3-12

soul, and occasionally it cost me. It cost me my fanciful notions, my self-serving dreams, my ideas about ministry, and any assumptions I held onto in ignorance about God's kingdom. It humbled and broke me at times while causing such a desperation in my soul that eventually receded into submission that always cried out, "Not my will, but yours, Lord."

I realized the way of a true disciple was about making me a real follower of Jesus. I could not be like the swine that stayed in a worldly pigpen or the independent goat that would take detours to partake of the bits and pieces of the world. I had to walk in my Christian life in order to walk it out by faith, ever following the Lord Jesus Christ into the unknown. My walk was bringing discipline to my spirit so I could hear what the Spirit was saying, whether in a small still voice or in the Word, as well as transforming my soul so that I could discern if a matter was of God.[43] It was obvious the Lord was trying to grow me up in my walk so that I could truly line up to His will.

Each time of testing revealed the depth of my flaws, exposing my character, and it was only as I came to a place of rest by faith that I saw the dawning of His light upon the terrain of my soul. Each time it became clearer to me the work of God that was being done in the darkness of the unknown.[44] At times it caused me to marvel, sometimes it overwhelmed me and at other times I would chide myself for making the walk harder instead of simply coming to a place of rest and enjoying the work being done in and around me.

Romans 6:1-8 became my outline. I had to die to sin and that required me to truly become identified with Jesus in His death and burial. When I received Jesus, I was positionally baptized in His death. In other words, I was immersed in His death and as a result, I was buried with Him. When the Father looked on me, He saw the life of His Son coming forth.

Death has to occur before there can be a resurrection. There are three types of deaths in this world. There is physical death where the body is put off, allowing the spirit and soul to be ushered into eternity,

---

[43] 1 Kings 19:11,12; Matthew 7:6; 25:32,33,41; Romans 12:1,2; 2 Corinthians 5:7
[44] John 1:4,5; Revelation 22:16

spiritual death where hope is cast to the side as one falls into hell, and there is death to the self-life where all matters of the flesh and the world are nailed to the cross so that the new man can be resurrected in a person. As believers, we are ever walking towards the demise of the physical body in order to become a martyr in this present age, a walking witness that is dead in the eyes of the world because of applying our personal cross.[45] The more we apply our personal cross to the "old man" to cross out the influence of the world upon the flesh, the more we are made alive by the life of Christ in us. As Jesus stated, "What does it profit a man if he gains the whole world but loses his own soul?"[46]

The more I became identified to Jesus, the more the new man was being worked in me. The Apostle Paul summarized it this way in Philippians 3:10, "That I may know him, and the power of his resurrection, and the fellowship of his sufferings, being made conformable unto his death." It simply comes down to the great exchange of the old for the new.

However, I also became more aware of the work of the kingdom of darkness as I came higher. It seemed that the higher I came in my Christian life, the greater the challenge became for me to discern and keep on guard against the wiles of the enemy. The enemy of my soul became more subtle and it required me to be more discerning of the spirit and environment around me. As the lion, Satan is looking for whom he may devour and as a swift leopard, he is quick to pounce on his prey at its most vulnerable times. Sometimes as Christians, we can become so comfortable or enthralled with the heights of God that we fail to see the great temptations that can come with such experiences. It is true we are enlarged on the mountaintops but we gain wisdom in the valleys of experiences where revelations must be walked out to become truths. It is easy to fall into the trap of testing all things according to mountaintop feelings, rather than testing the fruit it is truly producing in our attitudes and the relationships around us. [47]

---

[45] The word "witness" points to one who is a martyr.
[46] Matthew 16:26
[47] Matthew 7:16,20; 1 Corinthians 2:10-14; 2 Corinthians 2:11; 4:2-4; 1 Peter 5:8,9

The higher we come in our life in Christ, the more the Lord has to balance us out to keep us humble before Him. The Apostle Paul had a thorn in his side and I have had various challenges that have forever reminded me of my imperfections in order for me to remember who brings completion and perfection to a matter.[48]

Hindsight taught me that my failures in my initial Christian walk and my time at His table were to set me up for failure in the flesh so I could learn what it would mean to walk in the Spirit. The Spirit was always bringing an inward discipline to ensure a virtuous walk before the Lord. The inward disciplines also reminded me of the vital work of applying my personal cross.

Learning to be a disciple of Jesus brought me to low places to prepare me for high places so that I could effectively minister in the valleys of humiliation. The higher I went in the spirit, the more the gravity of this life brought me crashing back down to reality, causing weariness and depression. The lower God went into the depths of my soul with the cross, the higher I found myself soaring above the mountaintops of revelation. It was soaring above the mountains that I began to understand the great battle that is taking place in the unseen realm.

The reality is Satan wants to trip up each of us as believers no matter where we are in our Christian walk. On the mountaintops, pride and self-sufficiency can cause us to fall into Satan's traps. In the valleys drudgery and complacency can ensnare us, and in the canyons, despair, anger, and hopelessness can take us captive. The Bible tells us not to be ignorant of the devices of Satan, but the harsh reality is many Christians in America do not understand the great battle that is taking place.[49] They have become dulled down by the propaganda of the world, which takes away any edge of discernment.

The digression eventually becomes obvious. What was once considered abnormal (demonic) by God simply becomes uncomfortable to His people, but not unbearable. That which is uncomfortable to the conscience becomes justified, and if repentance does not occur, eventually such compromise will sear the conscience; and, evil that is

---

[48] 2 Corinthians 12:7-10
[49] 2 Corinthians 2:11; Ephesians 6:10-17

justified becomes a stench to God. At this stage, people have become blind to the dangerous state that surrounds them, and any challenge that might awaken them to the truth of their plight will simply cause them to rise up in anger and resistance.[50]

I looked back at my path and realized He had to first teach me to wait before Him, so secondly, I would be faithful to carry out His bidding regardless of the challenges; and, it was at this point of my life that He was teaching me the disciplines of following, being led, and walking in His Spirit. I did not understand it at the time, but He was teaching me how to stand by faith in who He is, withstand with the truth of His Word, and continue to stand because of His promises.[51] I should have recognized that such preparations were actual glimpses into the great challenges that were yet before me. As I have stated in the past, God never "wastes a good crisis."

I have recorded some of the events of my life during this period of growth, but what I realized is that through this time of growth, I found out who I was in the Lord. So many things had tried to define me in the past according to personal standards, religious notions, and various expectations. I found myself resentful towards standards, mocking when it came to notions, and angry at the expectations of others that always proved to be selfish and unrealistic. It took some real challenging situations and experiences, but I realized the only One I had to please and answer to was the Lord.

That simple truth set me free to know that my Creator knows who I am, and He alone is the One who can reveal what my potential is and my calling, and that He has designed a path before me that would allow me to discover all three points. Granted, I would have to become a struggling mountain climber at times, walk through some deep canyons until a way out was illuminated, and discover that the valleys were also a time of spiritual drought and purging. I also had some experiences with being brought down in the depths of the troubled waters, but the Lord

---

[50] Romans 1:21-32; 1 Timothy 4:1,2
[51] Romans 8:1, 14; Galatians 5:17,18; Ephesians 6:10-13; Hebrews 6:12

preserved me in such times until I was washed up on the shores of restoration.[52]

Ephesians 2:6 tells us, "And hath raised us up together, and made us sit together in heavenly places in Christ Jesus." Positionally every believer has been placed in those heavenly places in Christ, and it is from these heights that we gain a right perspective about God, as well as the Christian terrain that must be walked through and out daily by obedience. It is also from such heights we can catch glances into the spiritual battle that rages. This perspective is what enlarges and allows us to grow in our love and appreciation for our Lord.

I recognized that there is nothing worthwhile in me, this world or the life it offers. I needed to lay aside all those things that were besetting me from advancing forward in victory and coming higher in my life.[53] The more I discounted the value of the world and hated the need to exalt a somebody (me) out of a nobody (myself) to feel important and worthwhile, the more I discovered the life from above.

As long as our perspective is earthbound, we will be looking through the prisms of the flesh and the world, but once we are lifted above this world through identification in Christ and applying daily the personal cross to the "old man", we can begin to gain the heavenly perspective that will enlarge our understanding of our Lord, sharpen our eyes of faith to see beyond this world to the next, and discover the plans and works of the enemy.

The hindsight of wisdom gave me insight into the perfect ways of God while finetuning discernment to recognize what was happening around me, enabling me to realistically walk in light of what is yet to come. I began to see that the reason some Christians never reach the place where their love ceases to hide behind childish, worldly notions and fickle devotion in order to grow, is because they remain earthbound in their thinking and ways. They lack the courage to risk climbing the mountains, the endurance to see their way through the canyons, confidence towards the Lord in deep waters, and the necessary trust in the Lord to walk through the valleys. In essence, they lack faith towards

---

[52] Psalm 119;67, 71, 75; Isaiah 48:10
[53] Hebrew 12:1

the Lord because they fail to choose the way of faith to discover that He is who He says He is regardless of circumstances, crises, and trials.[54]

Each time I think about climbing the next mountain in front of me, I remember what Job 39: 27-29 says, "Doth the eagle mount up at thy command, and make her nest on high? She dwelleth and abideth on the rock, upon the crag of the rock, and the strong place. From thence she seeketh the prey, and her eyes behold afar off." At each mountain I had to face that I had come too far and experienced the beauty of too many mountaintops to settle for being an earthbound turkey that never gets far off the ground. I have been called to soar in the current of the Spirit, allowing me to dwell on the Rock, Jesus Christ, in a strong place where I am able to gain a heavenly perspective of the matters of earth, the battle in the spiritual realm, and to see even more so into the heart and love of God.

Come with Me

The dawn was coming and the shadows were fleeing. The Shulamite girl felt a stirring in her heart. She knew she was being called to come to a higher place with her beloved. It was exciting as well as daunting. She knew she was not being called to just any mountain. Myrrh means "bitter" and pointed to a type of death. It was one of six ingredients in the anointing oil that was used on sacrifices that designated and separated them as being acceptable to die.[55]

She recognized that for love to grow and remain acceptable to her beloved, every abyss that hid or contained her past notions about love had to be offered up and sacrificed. It was hard for her to let go of youthful notions but they had already caused a bitterness to her soul when darkness had come between her and her beloved. She realized the darkness was there because of the ignorance that comes with innocence. To hold onto innocence at this stage of her life would cause her to become emotionally inept, mentally stagnant, and stuck in the mire of childish silliness.

---

[54] Hebrews 11:6
[55] Exodus 30:22-31; Song of Solomon 4:6

Myrrh was also used as a medicine for deadening pain and purification. It would prove to be bitter to the taste, but when the plant was bruised a sweetness came out of it that could heal the soul as well as purge it.[56] She was aware that to avoid the bitterness, she had to allow that which was attached to her immature ideas of love to be crushed. The crushing would allow the real sweetness of her growing love to come forth.

The girl smiled as she remembered that it was not just the mountain of myrrh she was being called to, but the hill of frankincense. It was true that the mountain that stood before her was formidable, but after the mountain would be the lesser hill of frankincense. Frankincense was one of the five ingredients in the Holy Perfume.[57]

Frankincense pointed to "being white" or "righteousness. It was the most important of the aromatic gums since it could stand by itself as a perfume without any additions. Besides being a perfume, it could be used as medicine and an antidote to poison. She could see where her associations with the world had poisoned her relationship with the king, but now she was being prepared by the anointing of the oil to advance forward and by the sweet perfume to stand distinct.

She was also aware that to get frankincense from the tree, the husbandman had to make an incision in it.[58] It was clear that certain attitudes and practices of the flesh had to be crushed and cast to the side to allow the beautiful fragrance of the life in her to be emitted, but she also knew when fire was applied to the holy perfume that the fragrance of frankincense became more potent.

The Shulamite girl wondered what kind of fire would be applied to her life for her love to become even more special to her beloved. She was willing to experience whatever purging it would take to rid her of those things that would separate her from her beloved. He had told her that she stood pure before him, but she sensed that the terrain before

---

[56] A Dwelling Place for God, Ruth Specter Lascelle, pg. 224
[57] Exodus 30:34-38; Song of Solomon 4:6
[58] A Dwelling Place for God, Ruth Specter Lascelle, pgs. 232, 233

her would reveal other aspects of her character that might prove to be unpleasant.[59]

The king had required two things from her in the past and that was to rise up out of her circumstances, and the second was to come along with him in his circumstances. She rose up, but failed to walk with him. She had missed the opportunity to step in line with him and become identified in his life.

The fact that he was telling her to come with him from the mountain range of Lebanon showed that he wanted to lead her to elevated places with him, but what revealed to her that their relationship was taking on a new dimension is that for the first time he referred to her as, "my spouse." Clearly, she was no longer on trial and that he made his intentions known by referring to her as his spouse. She was now officially betrothed him.[60]

It was becoming obvious to her that her beloved was calling her above the influences of the world to a greater reality of him. She was overwhelmed by it all. The first place mentioned after Lebanon was Amana.[61] Amana was a mountain and it means "a covenant."[62] Yahweh always started from the highest point with a covenant to show His intentions towards and desires for His people. To start from Lebanon meant that she and her beloved were already starting from a high place of "right standing" before each other in their relationship, and his reference of her being his spouse confirmed it by pointing to a covenant of the heart, clearly showing his intention towards her.

The name he used for the next mountain was the Amorite name for "Mount Hermon."[63] Shenir means "snow mountain."[64] It was clear that challenges lay before them. Snow has a cleansing quality and provides water for the land, but it is also cold. Obviously, there needed to be more cleansing done in her life to ensure the purity of their relationship, but

---

[59] Song of Solomon 4:7
[60] Song of Solomon 4:8
[61] Ibid
[62] Smith's Bible Dictionary
[63] Song of Solomon 4:8
[64] Smith's Bible Dictionary

she also knew that love that loses heart in the midst of great trials can become cold and indifferent.

In the same sentence he mentioned "Mount Hermon." Hermon in Hebrew means "a peak, a summit." This mountain served as a special landmark for her people as well as marking their northern border.[65] It was clear that the reason for coming higher was to reach the peak of their potential in their love. Amazingly, the mountain had never been measured which brought to mind that love can't be measured. She realized that Hermon was just one peak and that from its perspective she would see that there were other mountains they would have to climb to reach even greater heights. She suspected each mountain would challenge her in different ways, but the peaks would enlarge her perspective and cause a desire to rise up in in her to also explore the heights of any future mountains that stood firmly in their path.

Her beloved reminded her that dangers lurk even in the mountains. There are the lions whose roar paralyzes those they seek to devour, and leopards that quietly stalk and wait for the unsuspecting and vulnerable prey that comes within reach of their cunningness and speed.[66] She needed to trust in his strength and wisdom when she heard the lion roar and she needed to keep alert and her eyes on him to avoid becoming prey.

Her beloved spoke to her again, making her heart leap with joy. "Thou hast ravished my heart, my sister, my spouse; thou has ravished my heart with one of thine eyes, with one chain of thy neck."[67] It was clear that his love for her was now consuming his heart and he even told her why for he could see her love for him when she looked at him. It was a glance for only him to see, but it spoke volumes to him of how her love for him possessed disciplines that strengthened it and made it more trustworthy. It was clear that her love would not wander from him again. He not only saw it in her eyes but in her countenance.

He further reinforced it when he called her "my sister, my spouse." The names reveal that in his eyes her place in his heart was being

---

[65] Ibid
[66] Song of Solomon 4:8
[67] Song of Solomon 4:9

enlarged. He first had invited her to come to his table, then he called her to come away with him, and now that she was willing to walk with him, he called her his spouse, one to whom he would share intimate matters with.

But, in this statement to her, he first called her, "sister." How precious was that word to her! Being a sister meant more than being betrothed to him. Being betrothed spoke of agreement, but being his sister implied she was now taking on his family's likeness, identifying her to his royal legacy. That legacy was not only a physical one but a spiritual one as well. For her people, the legacy entrusted to them carried an earthly inheritance, but what was more important is that it carried eternal promises with it. No doubt the two of them were about to discover some of the treasures attached to their legacy together.

Her betrothed goes on to confirm her place and position as he describes her love for him, "How fair is thy love, my sister, my spouse! How much better is thy love than wine! And the smell of thine ointments than all spices!"[68] Before she had delighted him in her initial innocence and unfeigned beauty, but now her love was delighting him.

Wine could be sweet to the taste but it also was used in the drink offerings. It was poured out on the ground before Yahweh.[69] He thought of her love being like an offering that once it was poured out would prove to be sweet to her beloved, and once fire was applied to the sweetness of her love it would also emit a fragrance that would even be enjoyed by heaven.

Her love had also disciplined what she would say, revealing wisdom. Instead of spouting off foolish ideas and demands because of a selfish, immature love, she now spoke those things that were sweet, bringing edification. Like honey her love had gone through a process, and now was desired by her beloved because it was not only sweet and sustaining to his soul but properly established, enabling it to stand during times of testing. He saw it to be better than any expensive ointment, as well as all the spices put together. Obviously, her love was distinct, anointed by sweetness brought out by the sacrifice of the old

---

[68] Song of Solomon 4:10
[69] Exodus 29:40,41; Leviticus 23:13, 18, 37; Numbers 15:5, 7, 10, 24

and the fire of the new, and as a result, it was being preferred by her beloved.[70]

His next statement caused joy to leap in her bosom, "A garden inclosed is my sister, my spouse; a spring shut up, a fountain sealed." She knew the garden pointed to her heart. In the past, the affections of her heart towards her beloved had been choked out by the many weeds that represented the cares of the world, and as a result it had become closed to his invitation; but, now her heart was closed to the world and becoming a garden where she and her beloved could fellowship. She would not allow anyone to partake of her water spring but her beloved, and until He uncapped the water like Jacob of old did for Rachel, the fountain would remain off limits to everyone else.[71]

The Shulamite girl could tell from her beloved's description of her garden that he understood what her love for him contained.[72] The word "plants" pointed to the work of resurrection and life, pomegranates to fruitfulness, the pleasant fruits to nourishment, the white, scented camphire to purity, the fragrant spikenard to preparation, the aromatic yellow saffron to flavoring and dye that enhances, the calamus, cinnamon, and myrrh to the anointing oil and frankincense to the holy perfume used in the tabernacle, along with aloes and chief spices that would enrich both their taste and smell. These ingredients had the ability to stir up her beloved as they partook of sweet fellowship, along with the desired fragrance that would attract and edify him.

Her garden was complete with all that would encourage pleasant and sustaining communion with her beloved. The fact that the fountain in her garden and the well that provided her garden with water received its waters from the pure streams of Lebanon reminded her that the waters were provided by the snow on Mount Hermon, and the streams brought and ensured continuous, ongoing life into the garden of her heart.[73]

---

[70] Song of Solomon 4:11
[71] Genesis 29:10-11; Song of Solomon 4:12; Matthew 13:7, 22; Colossians 3:2
[72] Song of Solomon 4;13,14
[73] Song of Solomon 4:15

She also realized that the water was not enough. It took the adverse winds of the north to establish the seed and the south wind to bring warm breezes for her garden to reproduce itself. She not only welcomed the adversity, but invited it as a type of prayer because she knew that the winds that followed would bring forth new life.[74]

It was clear to her that her heart was not hers any longer, it belonged to another, it belonged to her beloved. She wanted her garden to be a place where he could enjoy her and she could enjoy sweet communion with him as they partook of the growing love that was enriching both of their lives.

Her beloved honored her by saying, "I AM come into my garden, my sister, my spouse: I have gathered my myrrh with my spice: I have eaten my honeycomb with my honey; I have drunk my wine with my milk: eat, O friends."[75] It was clear that her beloved had enjoyed the beauty, the fragrance, and the fruits of her garden. He had uncapped the fountain to let the waters run, and in doing so he invited those who were his friends to partake of the fountain as well.[76]

She was happy that he wanted to share the precious water, fragrances, and fruits of the garden with his friends. She then heard another invitation. It was true that the garden was his, and he rightfully was the first one to partake of it. His invitation became clear that it was not only for him to enjoy and his friends to drink of, but she likewise needed to partake of it with him. After all, there was enough to go around, leaving her with not just some fruit or water, but an abundance of it. He acknowledged that very fact when he stated to her, "drink, yea, drink abundantly, O beloved."[77]

---

[74] Song of Solomon 4:16
[75] Song of Solomon 5:1
[76] Isaiah 12:2,3
[77] Song of Solomon 5:1

Follow Me
(The Second Companion)

Love had changed the slave girl into a woman of beauty and potential. She had not discerned the changes within herself until she had to realize how important her Lord had become to her. She had failed to see herself from his perspective, while failing to consider him in light of his selfless love and honorable character.

She had thought herself a slave while he saw a potential bride. She had seen herself as a substandard servant, while he saw her as one who would one day rule with him. She was content to sit at the table, while he desired for her to walk beside him when he was about the business of the kingdom.

Her frantic search for him caused her to reevaluate her attitude towards him. The reflection that looked back at her from the inner mirror of her heart had greatly humbled her. She realized she was assuming much about her position because of his love for her. She had failed to see its purity, thereby, perverting it. Her insidious suspicion towards him had downplayed his commitment towards her, providing an excuse for her to avoid making a real commitment towards him. He had invested much of himself in their times together, while she held onto certain rights to herself as a means to guard against rejection and betrayal.

Her unwillingness to trust his intentions towards her had caused her to become a restless wave that was emotionally tossed to and fro by personal changing moods that failed to silence her insecurities, bringing confusion and speculation.[78] She was unwilling for her love to be contained in a binding commitment thus avoiding steady, lasting consecration to her Lord. In the end, she was the one who ultimately rejected his love and betrayed his commitment to her.

As she thought about the garden where she had located him, she smiled to herself. She realized the garden represented her heart. When he first found her, her heart was broken and void of life, but it was

---

[78] Jeremiah 29:11; 1 Corinthians 14:33; Ephesians 4:14

because of his loving investment in a relationship with her that it began to take on life.[79]

It was true that the cold unrelenting north winds of her past had caused her to become as dead, hidden away in some lifeless pit, but it was the sweet south winds of her Lord's love that revived what seemed dormant and lifeless in order to bring forth lasting life.

She couldn't count the times her Lord had invited her to partake of the precious waters of his kingdom. She had been thirsty, but in the beginning, she had only taken sips of the refreshing water here and there. It was true, its sweetness and freshness caused her to drink more and more of it. It had dawned on her the night she had sought him that partaking of the waters was like priming the pump, uncapping living waters in her own soul. It became clear that she would never be content with any other water. She was acutely aware that the waters came from a fountain that found its source in the heavenly and the eternal.[80]

The waters had brought life to her and now there were fruits and sweet spices dotting the landscape of her soul. The fruits of his love had produced an inner character in her that was manifesting itself in the form of virtues that were pleasant to her Lord as well as to her. The spices emitting from the inner life that was being formed in her by their relationship were like sweet graces that spoke of meekness clothing her with the beauty of salvation. In the humility of this meekness she had been lifted up to know satisfaction as mercy and truth came together causing the confusion to flee and righteousness and peace would touch in a sweet array.[81]

Her Lord had told her what his intentions were towards her from the beginning. He was seeking a bride the day he found her, and inwardly she was seeking one who would save her. He was willing to prepare her to be a bride, and she was willing to be saved, but being his bride had brought much anxiety to her as she began to realize the high calling of her status and the extent of the commitment that was necessary to fulfill her obligations.

---

[79] Luke 4:18
[80] Isaiah 12:2,3; John 4:14; 7:37-39
[81] Psalm 85:9-11; 149:4; Matthew 5:5

The night she desperately sought her Lord had caused her to face some unpleasant realities about her own intentions toward him. She wanted such a commitment with someone special, but not until she had tasted the finer things of the world. She had prayed for such a relationship, but not until she experienced the heights of romance and was assured of a union that would prove to be a "forever honeymoon."

The light of his love had exposed the darkness of her immature notions. His goodness had served as a mirror to her silliness, and his steady commitment towards her revealed how fickle she was in her commitment towards him.

The garden is what brought the greatest indictment against her. She realized that the beauty of the garden of her heart was the result of being nurtured by him in their relationship. The beauty was simply the reflection of his goodness. The aromatic spices that emitted fragrance from her life were because of the investment of his love. The sweetness of the fruits was because of him cultivating the ground of her heart in times of sweet communion.

It was clear that her Lord had opened up her heart, and without her realizing what he was doing, her Lord had planted various flowers and spices in the ground of her heart to grace her life and times of fellowship with him. He alone had watered the garden and set a fountain of blessings in the midst of it. The awareness of his work revealed that her heart now belonged to him.

The new revelation overwhelmed her. She thought she was determining the extent of his impact on her heart, mind, and life when in reality he was capturing her heart, setting the tone of her affections, and changing the terrain of her mind.

His voice broke through, "Follow me." This time she would not hesitate, she would follow him. She was pleased that he led her back to the garden of fellowship, but was aware that there were others present. At first, she was confused, and then she realized that those in the garden had been invited by her Lord.

As she walked through the garden beside him, he greeted others and smiled as each one complimented him on the beauty, fragrance, and fruitfulness of the garden. It was clear they were seeing her Lord's investment, smelling the fragrance of his commitment, and tasting the sweetness of the fruitfulness of the garden. It began to dawn on her that what they were being complimentary about was that they were seeing the result of her Lord's investment. In essence, they were seeing his likeness in her.

Clearly, she was now identified with him in a special way. She had taken on his likeness in such a way that she was being personally identified to his name, his household, and his kingdom.

She recognized that even though it was her garden, it was his to share with others. He had prepared her for this time and this place. Her life and his work in her heart were no longer to be hidden away, and her Lord now invited those hungry and thirsty to come and partake of the fruit of her garden.

As she observed his generosity towards those in the garden, he turned to her. His smile was like the sun breaking forth upon the landscape, his eyes shining like the glimmering rays dancing across the waters, and his countenance was soft like the petals of a white rose.

The words that followed caused her to realize that he recognized that her love towards him had come to a higher place of maturity, "What do you think of our garden, my cherished one, my beloved?"

Transforming Love

The Battle

The Christian life is wrought with various tests. Each test will reveal the character of one's faith. Faith is established and confirmed based on the inner character of the person. The greatest test for inner character has to do with faithfulness.

I really did not understand true faithfulness. We often hear the word, "faithfulness" in relationship to marriage. In fact, faithfulness is a vow that both the man and woman make to each other in such a union. However, faithfulness is one of the ingredients of the fruit of the Spirit.[1] It has to do with being faithful with such things as keeping your word, seeing all commitments through to the end, being honorable in all activities, and making sure talents are utilized in a constructive way to advance forward the integrity of all matters that you are involved with.

In my younger years, I thought I was faithful for the most part, but I found out that what I thought was faithfulness was misdirected loyalty. I discovered that I often responded to a matter, not because it was the right thing to do, but because I was being pressured emotionally, intellectually, and spiritually to do it as a means to keep a type of quasi peace. This attempt was to keep the monsters of others' selfishness at bay, as well as the dragons of unmerciful judgments which created guilt and rejection to rise up in me, while mocking me as I attempted to hold back the tidal waves of personal frustration that were erupting in my soul. Making a decision under pressure was not a choice but a reaction to the environment around me, and such reaction often caused resentment and anger, two ingredients that were not of the Holy Spirit.

I began to understand that faithfulness was about choosing what was right and true regardless of the amount of pressure being put on me by others to comply. Each right decision lined me up to heaven, enabling me to remain true to my heart, while maintaining the integrity

---

[1] Galatians 5:22,23

of my calling, and allowing me to look in the mirror without feeling like a hypocrite.

I sincerely thought I had character, but discovered I was simply a character who thought myself to be wise. As the Lord graciously revealed the quality of my inner character, I realized I possessed no real godly character and that the only way I would ever acquire it was by letting it be forged in me. However, this required me to make right choices according to my faith towards the Lord that often proved contrary to my selfish feelings, fleshly desires, and worldly hopes.

At times the battles that often forged my character were intense. The first real battle of my faith revealed that my reliance was on the world while God served as my option, simply a backup when the world failed me. I had failed to see that my life was marked by the failures of the world, but the problem is the world always provided various options to me, creating the false hope and illusion that the right answer was around the next bend, over the next hill, or waiting on the other side of the mountain.

The problem is if you believe the world to be the solution and the Lord your option, you will naturally run down one optional rabbit trail after the other until you have exhausted them all. Then you have to question why, as a believer, did I avoid choosing the only real and lasting solution?

In time the answer became obvious to me. We avoid the only solution, God, because it takes all of the control out of our hands to pick and choose according to our own whims. When there is only one solution, you must wait on the one solving the problem, and often God is never quick enough in our minds in solving the problem that is demanding our immediate attention to avert complete disaster.

Hindsight often revealed that waiting on the Lord was all about preparation. I sat before the Lord waiting to hear His voice, and once I heard His voice, I stood before Him waiting for Him to open the right door. However, this is when I found the challenge behind real waiting taking place. At first, I thought that once I heard His voice the matter was a done deal, only to discover it was a work in progress and the work in progress was my faith.

Once I stood still, I thought the door would immediately open, but I found that the closed door ended up mocking me for waiting when there were other doors I could at least try; however, I also knew from past experiences that any attempts to open them would be nothing but an exercise in futility as I breathlessly beat against them. I wrestled before the Lord about the closed door until I was exhausted and conceded, "Not my way but your way." The longer the door remained shut, the more I had to refrain from giving way to hopelessness and despair by trusting Him with the details and admitting, "Not my timing but yours." At times I found myself becoming desperate, and pushed back the flood of anxiety while trying to maintain some semblance of sanity, only to end up surrendering to, "Not my will but Yours."[2]

In my struggles with waiting, I often reminded myself of Isaiah 40:29-31, "He giveth power to the faint; and to them that have no might he increaseth strength. Even the youths shall faint and be weary, and the young men shall utterly fall: But they that wait upon the LORD shall renew their strength; they shall mount up with wings as eagles: they shall run, and not be weary; and they shall walk, and not faint." I reminded myself that in waiting before the Lord, I was being prepared to walk out my Christian life and calling with authority and power. Each point of concession, each decision to trust Him, and every place of surrender brought me to a place of rest in Him and His sovereignty, quietly trusting that He would faithfully bring about that which would be perfected, effective, and eternal in my life.

The Lord never disappointed me in my different adventures in the valleys, during my various climbing experiences, and in the deepest parts of despairing canyons. It was clear that He was growing me up, refining my faith, forging character in my inner being, and always preparing me to come higher.

I also was aware that He was enlarging and refining my testimony. When I started out, I was excited about my salvation, and after I was brought down on my face in brokenness and repentance, I was excited about His incredible love, forgiveness, and care in my life. As the confusing walls of my perception came down, I became more excited

---

[2] Lamentations 3:25,26; Matthew 26:36-42

124

about Him. I could see that the Lord was directing my affections from earthly things and experiences to Himself.[3]

It was clear that I started out as a lost soul seeking a Savior and a mournful sinner looking for forgiveness, but eventually I graduated to a child trying to discover her place in God's family, and from there a struggling Christian desiring greater heights in Christ, on to a believer attempting to be pliable before the Spirit in order to be placed in His church and prepared as part of His bride, while becoming a faithful servant who was effectively serving in His household. I knew that Jesus was to be my source, but I needed to make Him my all in all, my consuming reality.[4] I had to let Him take His rightful place in every area of my life. I knew by letting Him take His rightful place in every area of my life it would affect and change my attitude to ensure I properly responded to Him.

After considering all my past disastrous detours, I remember thinking to myself. "When all is said and done, I want my Lord to be able to say, 'Well done my good and faithful servant." I knew that if He was going to entrust me with more, I had to be faithful with those small things that were in front of me.[5] I knew to be faithful I had to deny myself up front and make it about what was right to the Lord regardless of how I felt or what was going on. It became clear that to be faithful, I needed to make the Lord and His concerns and business my first and foremost obligation.

One day a woman who operated in the "word of knowledge," looked at me and told me that I wanted to be acknowledged as His faithful servant, but the Lord wanted to call me friend."[6] I can't tell you how much her insightful statement affected me. I was emotionally overwhelmed and greatly humbled. I silently sat while her words penetrated my understanding and began to flood my soul.

I knew that Jesus wanted to call His followers friends, but I was trying to simply become a faithful servant. It later struck me that if I could be a

---

[3] Colossians 3:2
[4] Colossians 3:11
[5] Matthew 25:21-23; Luke 16:10
[6] 1 Corinthians 12:8

faithful servant, I could also be a faithful friend. As a servant I was simply entrusted with obligations, but as a friend the Lord could entrust me with the matters of His heart.[7] Needless to say, I didn't feel worthy to be called His friend, but in all honesty, I was not worthy to be His servant either.

As believers we are given pinnacle moments in our lives when we are lifted up out of the valleys and firmly placed on a mountain peak so we can see how far the Lord has brought us. It's at those times we are allowed to see the purpose for our challenges. For me, I realized the Lord was preparing me to be a trustworthy friend that He could entrust with deep matters.

It was then that I learned some lessons about faithfulness. True faithfulness is sensitive to the one it is directed towards. Due to sensitivity, it has the ears to hear and since it is pure, it has the ability to properly discern how to hear in order to do what is honorable. It is not enough to hear someone; you must be able to discern what is being said.

Jesus warned that we must beware of how we hear things, because the way we process it can be perverted and wrong.[8] It takes a type of purity to discern and hear something properly. Discernment involves first getting self out of the way so that one can hear what the Spirit is saying in regard to a matter.

Looking back, I could see how the challenges, crises, and pressures forced me to keep spiritually sharp so I could discern what was going on in order to be faithful to the Lord. However, when the pressure of life's challenges was missing, that is when I discovered how quickly faithfulness can wane. At such times this virtue becomes an assumed quality rather than a practicing reality.

The alertness of my faithfulness depended on me recognizing the weakness of my own character and holding the line of righteousness for myself. It was when things were running smooth or I found myself in a whirlwind of ministry activities that I unknowingly became complacent

---

[7] John 15:13-16
[8] Luke 8:18

towards the things of God, allowing assumptions to give me a false sense of what was happening around me.

There was a situation where I made a decision, assuming the Lord would agree with me. It seemed right and felt right, but I later discovered that I allowed my responsibility to slide to the wayside as I conceded it to another individual. It turned out to be a disaster which caused me to repent for handing the reins the Lord had entrusted to me to someone else. I certainly learned some important lessons, one being that faithfulness towards the Lord entails being faithful to my calling and position in Him. I was not to make an assumption that because something looked right to me that it was right before the Lord.

Once I was so busy with ministry that Jesus ceased to be the focus of my life and activities. I assumed He was the center of my activities because it was ministry, only to discover He was missing in all of it. I ended up weary and without any strength to even continue down the path.

Assumption in ministry will turn into a type of complacency that is shored up by presumption that all must be well because how could such activities be wrong?[9] During that time, I discovered how easy it is to become complacent towards the matters of God in the midst of business. Even "good" things can become "stumblingblocks" and the "best" can fail to lead to excellence. All of my business had robbed me of physical strength, permitting weariness to consume my soul, while allowing complacency to gain a foothold, causing me to lose my spiritual edge. In this state, I failed to discern where I was and where I was heading.

Once you lose your edge, you begin to slip into a quasi-state that eventually makes everything appear surreal and untrustworthy. I had left my first love standing in my rear-view mirror, forgetting who was the source of my strength.[10] The ordeal ended with me finding myself contending with a major health crisis, as well as a crisis of faith that once again caused me to seek out the Lord and to fling myself on Him.

---

[9] Revelation 3:14-19
[10] Revelation 2:4

When one becomes complacent towards the Lord, the first thing that slips is discernment, followed by maintaining the ways of righteousness which becomes a point of unfaithfulness. I had become unfaithful and ineffective in my ways because I had become half-hearted towards the real matters of the Lord and casual about my relationship with Him. It all had been replaced with the activities of ministry.

Ministry is to be the byproduct of the Christian life, and it is not meant to be its ultimate goal. My misguided assumptions about the place and part ministry was to play in my life caused me to lose my bearings, my passion, my joy, and my strength as I became consumed by darkness. The Lord allowed me to physically, mentally, and spiritually slide into a type of grave where once again I had to come back to center as to who He is and who He needs to be. I had to line up my priorities to Him, renew and refine my vision according to Him, and repent for foolishly leaving Him behind.

I knew what it felt like to be lost and hopeless, as well as uncertain and having a leanness in the spirit, but the spiritual darkness of what became a type of grave to me caused a desperation I had never experienced before. I could trace the different stages of my Christian walk where I made some major missteps, but this was not a misstep but a major fall into a dark abyss.

In the darkness I began to think about my missteps and what I had learned from them. The first mistake in my walk happened when I had settled for knowledge of Jesus instead of knowing Him. In the second misstep I had assumed that since something seemed right it would be alright with the Lord without praying about it and truly seeking His will. In this situation I assumed that ministry was the essence of the Christian walk. Each assumption hid the fact that Jesus was missing from the equation.

We often learn the same lesson over and over because the terrain varies, the situation may be new, and the challenges diverse. As a result, we fail to discern that the one thing that has not changed is the test—what have we done or what are we doing with Jesus? Are we neglecting fellowship with Him because we assume that He is with us in all we do? Are we presuming He is in a matter because it seems right to our religious conscience or is a point of ministry, thereby, we fail to faithfully seek His face in prayer and wait upon Him until we have an audience with Him to know His will about something? It is when we line up to His will, we can make sure we are in step with Him when it comes to all ministry.

The problem with each misstep is that it will cause us to be ineffective and we will find that we are walking contrary to the ways of God. We do not realize that each point of temptation becomes more subtle because it is geared to always take our focus off of our Lord and lead us down a path that ends in vanity.

Each failure or misstep on my part caused the consequences to escalate for me. For example, in my first initial encounter with Jesus He came to me to forgive and save me by taking care of the burden of sin. In my second encounter, He came to me in my brokenness to bring restoration, but in the third situation, I had to arise and seek Him out to once again come into communion with Him. However, the darkness of the grave brought sobering trepidation to me. I sensed that He was going deeper in me, and that regardless of how desperate I was to see a resolution to the matter, the darkness would not easily part until the work was finished.

Missed Opportunity

The Shulamite girl was ready to bid the light of the day goodbye as she prepared herself to settle in for the night. There had been a lull after her last fellowship with the king in the garden. The sweetness of their fellowship was becoming a bit like the twilight on the terrain of the countryside, as the memories of it were now silhouettes that danced around the outer courts of her mind.

She relished this time of the evening because it signaled the day was over. During the day, she had unselfishly poured out her energies and talents as she faced the demands of the world and carried out her dutiful fleshly responsibilities. She had washed her feet to make sure she had dealt with the defilement of the day's worldly, fleshly activities. After all, she had to walk through the world and there was no way that she was immune from its influences. The washing of her feet freed her from any lingering defilement of the world, ensuring that her spirit would be at peace and her soul in a state of rest.[11]

Since the horizon was void of any expectation of future interruptions and visitations, she had taken off her worldly garments in preparation for the night. Now she could slip into a comfortable mode that catered to her particular mood, allowing her to slide into a state of relaxation that would enable her to succumb to sleep.

As sleep began to carry her to the furthest abyss where she could disconnect from her surroundings, a voice began to penetrate the darkness, parting the depths of the slumber that was upon her soul.[12] It touched her heart and began to awaken her spirit. It was clear that the voice was familiar and was trying to arouse her from her indifferent state. She struggled to connect with the reality of this intrusion. As the darkness parted and the foggy cloud of slumber dissipated, she recognized the voice of her beloved.

She was somewhat taken aback by the timing of his intrusion. Clearly, he had not come to her as king. As king, he always met her in the day where some type of pomp and circumstance would announce his arrival. It dawned on her that he had probably come as a shepherd in the night. She could only speculate that he had come at that particular time after tending to the flock. As a responsible shepherd, He would first make sure that each sheep was taken care of and properly contained within the makeshift sheepfold on the outer skirts of the community, leaving a porter to guard the door so as to prevent any sheep to wander away from the rest of the flock and become lost in the night.

The Shulamite girl didn't only hear his voice, but he began to knock, confirming his presence at her door. As the foggy cloud lifted from off her soul, she heard him speak, "Open to me, my sister, my love, my dove, my undefiled: for my head is filled with dew, and my locks with the drops of the night."[13]

Although they were betrothed, he had not yet come to her on a permanent basis, nor did he have the right to walk into her abode without

---

[11] John 13:4-10
[12] Song of Solomon 5:2
[13] Ibid

her invitation. It was clear that the term, "sister" revealed that he was seeking the refuge of a family member, where he could find shelter from the night, shake the dew off of his hair, and stay until the sun once again warmed the countryside.

By the terms he used to address her, she could tell that his love was the same for her, and that he recognized her focus on their relationship had not wavered. He also was eluding to the fact that she had kept herself separate from the world. However, she sensed there might be a deeper message in his sentence, but the subtle impression quickly vanished as she focused on her present state. Her reply was swift, "I have put off my coat; how shall I put it on? I have washed my feet; how shall I defile them?"[14]

Her beloved's response exposed the utter selfishness of her reply. He put his hand by the hole of the door.[15] It was a reminder that he was quick to reach out to her when she was considered defiled, but she was too concerned with her present state to respond to his voice and his knocks on the door. He had sought her behind lattices and walls but she was too self-centered about her own undefiled state to even open the door for him to come in from the night air. He had served her at banqueting tables, but she was unwilling to let him in so she could serve him after a day in the pastures with his sheep followed by a journey through the night air to see her.

She suddenly felt a strong conviction sweep across her conscience as it spiraled downward to abruptly land in the pit of her stomach.[16] She had taken such pride to keep herself right for the next meeting with her beloved, but because his visitation had proved to be inconvenient to her, she squandered the opportunity to open the door and let him in so she could simply serve him.

Her response to the conviction was decisive. She rose up to open the door to him, but as she reached for it she realized that the oils she had used on her body and hands to preserve her beauty in the

---

[14] Song of Solomon 5:3
[15] Song of Solomon 5:4
[16] Ibid

challenging heat of the land was even a greater indictment against her.[17] She had faithfully prepared herself to meet with him outwardly by doing various rituals, but her initial response revealed that selfishness still resided in aspects of her character. It was becoming obvious to her that in the right situation she was inwardly unprepared to meet him. The oil that fans the flame of her affections within was limited by her selfishness. Here she had been preparing herself for a meeting with him in the garden, but her self-interest prevented her from meeting him when he unexpectedly came to her abode, seeking a place from the night air to actually spend time with her.

How foolish she had been in her initial selfish response. She had been preparing to advance their relationship, only to take on a casual and unresponsive pose towards his visitation when it interrupted her sleep. She had kept the night lights burning for her comforts, but had failed to keep them lit in the dark of the night for him.

She had to open the door and set matters right. It did not matter if she was ready for the night, but what counted is if she was ready to respond to her beloved regardless of the time and place. After all, real love is not about what is convenient but what is right, honorable, and moral. Preparation is not about moments, but being ready in all seasons. It was easy to be ready in the season of expectation to commune with the one she loved in the garden, but there were other seasons where complacency could easily set it. It was becoming clear to her that in the seasons of spiritual inactivity, the greatest test of one's love and character could come, and she needed to be prepared to faithfully respond to any of his unexpected visitations in the night.

When she managed to opened the door, her beloved had withdrawn.[18] She stood still, trying to grasp what had happened. Surely the space of time between his knocking on her door and her opening it was minimal. He could have waited for her to respond, but then she realized she had not given him any reason to wait. Her initial verbal response implied that it was not worth her time to put her coat back on before letting him in. She didn't ask him to wait; rather, she rejected his

---

[17] Song of Solomon 5:5
[18] Song of Solomon 5:6

overtures by expressing that she had no desire to open the door in her present state.

She had thought herself to be more mature in her love for him, but now she was facing the harsh reality of how self-centered her love remained. She had assumed he would understand that her response was not of rejection, yet how could it be taken in any other light? She had presumed that he would ask her to set another time convenient for her, but his activities didn't necessarily allow for such luxuries. As a shepherd, his foremost commitment was to the welfare of the sheep; therefore, it was up to her to adjust her time to him.

Her presumption that he would automatically seek a better time according to her schedule reminded her that such presumptions are what causes one to walk right past the door of opportunity. When her people were in the wilderness they failed to enter into the Promised Land when presented with the open door of opportunity to do so. Their unbelief caused them to reject opportunity, slamming the door to what was to be their inheritance from Yahweh. They had assumed their Creator would adjust to what they perceived to be justifiable rebellion, while failing to recognize that their response had justly provoked Him to anger. The judgment was passed down: the present generation would not enter the Promised Land. After hearing the consequences, some of the people took another wrong turn by presuming that if they tried to obey Yahweh that He would let bygones be bygones, but the door was shut to His blessings. Instead of meeting with Yahweh's blessing, they tasted the bitterness of the sword and death.[19]

Perhaps her foolishness was on a minor scale but it was as serious and devastating to her as it was to her people so many years ago. By keeping her door shut, she had failed to walk through the door of opportunity to commune with her beloved and serve him at her table. She called out to him in the darkness, but was met with silence—silence that sucked the remaining expectation from her soul.[20] The silence mocked her as she became aware that her first response centered

---

[19] Numbers 14:1-38; 2 Peter 2:10
[20] Song of Solomon 5:6

around her. Clearly, there was an element of emotional fickleness remaining in her affections for her beloved.

The Shulamite girl at that moment realized that it was her beloved that held her heart and without him, life would elude her, love would mock her, and darkness would consume any real hope and expectation for a meaningful life. She had to find him, and without coat or sandals, she ran blindly out into the night to seek him. She had to right the wrong she had done to him. She had to make her beloved understand that regardless of her complacency towards his request, that it was not rejection of him, and that she valued him, prized their love, and now realized that she desired him more than her very breath.

When she encountered the watchmen, she was in the wrong attire, unprotected and open to misunderstanding and abuse. They couldn't understand why a woman of her position was in such a state. They had no time for what appeared to be nonsense to them, and no patience to hear her explanation. They had expected better conduct and presentation from her, and were not about to show pity on her. They were harsh in their judgments of her, rough with her in their accusations, and aggressive towards her as they pushed her to the side. The keeper of the gate showed the same regard towards her as he stripped the veil away from her, leaving her more exposed to the night elements.[21]

In the past she had easily found her beloved, but the abuse and the stripping she experienced caused more confusion. Where was her beloved and who could help her find him? Clearly, the men watching over the city and its gates were not open and willing to help her. There was only one recourse and that was to turn to the maidens of the city and charge them with keeping an eye out for her beloved. If they encountered him, she wanted them to tell him how she was sick of heart because of her failure to show him the love he rightfully deserved.[22]

The first time she was in this situation was because she was being overwhelmed by being in the presence of his love, but now desperation consumed her because he had withdrawn himself from her and was

---

[21] Song of Solomon 5:7
[22] Song of Solomon 5:8

nowhere to be found.[23] She knew her present state was due to her complacency towards their relationship, her selfish assumptions and foolish presumptions about his love, and she suspected these inexperienced handmaidens didn't know the whereabouts of her beloved, but unlike the watchmen and the gatekeeper, they at least heard the desperation in her charge and took time to enter in with her.

As the maidens stood about her, she was asked a question that made her realize a simple truth, that the important matters of the heart and life are often taken for granted due to assumptions and presumptions. What we take for granted we often become complacent towards, and once complacency sets in, we will fail to see the importance of it until we lose it.

Her desperation to find her beloved had stirred up their curiosity, inspiring them to ask the question that not only unlock the corridors of her mind, but the secret chambers of her heart. "What is thy beloved more than another beloved, O thou fairest among women? What is thy beloved more than another beloved, that thou dost so charge us?"[24]

Keeping the Home Fires Going
(The Second Companion)

The bride-to-be had just finished some of the business of the day. She had taken a more active role in the activities of her Lord's household since that night when she had to seek him. She had even begun to settle into a routine. She knew that her Lord was out in the fields, overseeing his flocks and assumed he would spend another night in the field or in a near-by village.

She also knew that he took special interest in every lamb, ewe, and ram, which required a great deal of time. It was not the number of sheep that counted as much as the quality of their well-being. He wanted to make sure his shepherds were responsible, the pasture land good, the waters pure, and the environment safe so that the sheep could thrive.

---

[23] Song of Solomon 2:6
[24] Song of Solomon 5:9

Her routine in the household caused her to become comfortable in her position. She felt good about her involvement and activities to keep the household running during his absence. Some days seemed longer than others but she was clearly coming to terms with her role.

She prepared for the night earlier than usual. She was rewarding herself after what she considered to be a good day's work. She felt she had the right to cater to her personal desires and whims. She had taken a longer bath than usual, pampered her skin with certain lotions, did a manicure, and had settled into bed with a good book that would cause rest to come to her soul.

And rest did come, as sleep enfolded her like a warm blanket. She had drifted off into a pleasant state when all of a sudden, she heard a voice intrude into her slumber, followed by a knock. She couldn't imagine who would rudely disturb her at a time such as this, unless it was some type of emergency. Her heart leaped at the thought as fear began to peek around the outer edges of confusion. She realized there was no urgency to the voice that remained low and appeared close to a whisper.

It was then that she was able to distinguished the voice as being her Lord. She was somewhat taken aback because he had never come to her bedroom door before.[25] All interactions in the past had been at the table or in the garden but never in this way. After all, she was not prepared to receive him in her bed chamber.

Her response was curt as she told him she was in bed for the night. She couldn't see him, but she sensed a certain sadness permeate through the door as he silently stood before it. It dawned on her that he had come in from the night seeking fellowship with her and she was too full of herself to be concerned with the one who had redeemed her from a life of slavery. He had given all and she didn't have it in her to step over her silly rights, and pass over a little inconvenience in order to meet with him in fellowship. He had ensured her the best and she couldn't even take a little time to serve him when he was tired after long days in the fields.

---

[25] Revelation 3:20

She had thought that she was past the foolishness of her selfishness, but all of a sudden, she came face to face with it and it made her repulsed. She felt her heart sink as she recognized the terrible mistake she made, the opportunity she missed, and the love that failed to respond because selfishness was sitting on the throne.

She ran to the door only to find that he was no longer there. As she touched the door, she thought of that gentle hand that had knocked on it, bringing greater conviction, causing nausea to sweep across her stomach as the knot in it tightened once again. She had noted that his hands were scarred. When she asked what happened, he simply smiled. She later learned the scars pointed to a time of great conflict that had taken place between his kingdom and that of another. As he stood in the gap, he was the one who was wounded. [26]

The woman wondered how many times would she be tested at the same place and fail because her love for him took a back seat to her foolishness. How many times would she exalt activities over fellowship with him before learning that there is no substance to life without him? How many times did she have to sense his disappointment due to her selfishness of demanding certain rights over spending time with him before she would finally get her priorities right by placing her Lord at the head of those priorities and making service to him her main agenda at all times and in all situations?

The words, "How many times," echoed in her mind as she asked herself a simple question, "Why can't you get it right?" She had been so busy keeping the home fires going for when he returned that she failed to keep the fire alive in her heart so that she would be prepared to respond the minute she recognized his voice. She wanted a place of comfort for him to come to, but was not prepared to offer personal comfort of service to him when the opportunity presented itself. He sought her fellowship and she sought an excuse. He wanted to see her upon his arrival home and she wanted to put off seeing him until it was convenient for her.

It was true she was ordained to be his bride, but she was still in the position of servitude with the responsibility of ultimately pleasing him. As

[26] Isaiah 53:5; John 20:25-27; Revelation 1:7

a servant, she was to be a watchman ready to always stand watch over the matters affecting their relationship and the household. As a bride waiting for him to come to her and for her, she had to be ready at all times to respond to his voice or his knock. As one who was part of the household, she was to be in the mode of preparation to receive him regardless of the time, day, or hour, and she had miserably failed in all three arenas.[27]

It was clear that she had allowed her love for her Lord to become stagnant in the midst of daily activities. She was so busy doing, she forgot to keep her heart tender and sensitive towards him. She valued what she did, but forgot it was to maintain an environment that would be pleasing and beneficial to her Lord. She was pleased with what she had accomplished in his household, but was not ready to give of herself and fulfill the real calling of her position as his bride to bring pleasure to him in sweet fellowship.

She was aware that she could stand there and slide into a vacuum that held no answer, or she could seek after him and once again repent of her inaction. She could fall at his feet and admit she was a hopeless case, while keeping in mind that his love always made her hopeful. After all, grace was the glue that kept his love towards her rich. It contained new compassions and mercies every day that kept it present and applicable and it was enduring because it always proved to be longsuffering during her failures, faithful when she was faithless, and forgiving when she sought it.[28]

It was then that she realized it was his love for her that had always given her confidence to approach him regardless of how pathetic she had been in her responses. She became overwhelmed by the urgency to seek him out to bring about reconciliation to restore what had already been established. She had to right her wrong so she could advance forward in a relationship with him, to continue to experience the freedom of his love.

She ran out into the night in search of him. She was familiar with the terrain but in the darkness of night the shadows confused her and the

---

[27] Matthew 24:42-46; 25:1-13; Revelation 3:20
[28] Lamentations 3:22-24; 2 Timothy 2:13; 1 John 1:9

obstacles before her caused fear and sometimes hesitation, but she knew that the darkness was the consequence of her inaction, the obstacles reminders of her foolishness, and her uncertainty firmly lay at the feet of her own selfishness after she squandered her right to stand before her Lord in service and communion.

She encountered some of the individuals that had dealings with her Lord. They had seen her in the garden with him and certainly they would have some knowledge of his whereabouts. As she approached them to enquire of his whereabouts, they immediately took offense towards her because it was clear she was not in the proper attire or in the right setting for them to give her any consideration. Their speech became rough towards her and their mannerisms aggressive as they began to push her away and shove her to the side as they went about their activities. They mocked her as they moved past her, leaving her to stand alone.

As she was trying to quiet the confusion of her soul, the gate keeper of her Lord's household had witnessed her interaction with the elders of the city and saw his opportunity in her vulnerable state to even heap more ridicule and shame upon her. These reactions caused much confusion. Did they not know her relationship with the Lord? Did they think because of her attire she had been rejected or thrown out of the household to be discarded like a garment that had suddenly lost it's beauty and purpose.

She was speculating, but she realized they had to be assuming and presuming much about her like the priest Eli had done with the despairing Hannah.[29] The former slave girl was not out in the night because she had been thrown out of the house, but because she was seeking the Lord of the household, the one she was betrothed too.

She wondered how these very same individuals would have reacted if they understood her real mission. One mention of the situation to her Lord, and these men would find themselves having to stand before him and give an account for their unbecoming actions.[30] As she looked down at herself, she realized that she didn't look the part of a bride to be. She was exposed because of her attire and now sullied by her interaction

---

[29] 1 Samuel 1:9-17
[30] 1 Peter 5:1-4

with those who were to be watchmen of the city. It was then that she became aware of the shadows taking on forms, living forms.

Obviously, there were others who had witnessed her exchange and were beginning to move from the cover of darkness. She knew that she stood as a spectacle in front of them, but at that moment she didn't care.[31] Perhaps those who lived in the shadows of the night had witnessed where her Lord had gone.

She boldly asked them if they had seen the Lord of the household, the king of the kingdom. As they gathered around her, she could see that some were curious about her, while others had a question mark forming on their face. It was apparent they knew of her Lord and understood he was also king, but it was not the Lord that was the center of their attention at that moment, but her.[32]

Finally, one of the observers allowed the question that had formed in his mind to be expressed, "Why are you here?"

"I'm looking for my Lord," she responded.

"At this time?" another asked.

"Yes, he parted without some matters being resolved," she quietly answered.

Some shook their heads as another made this statement in lieu of a question. "We remember you. You were once like us, living in the shadows of the day as a slave until your Lord bought you. We have watched you become one who now walks freely in the light. What makes him so important to you that you would risk coming out at this time when the darkness of suspicion is upon the minds of even those who are to oversee the welfare of this city?"

The statement and question set her back. She no longer was a slave, hidden in the shadows of indifference and covered by the darkness of oppression. Until now she never thought about others taking note of her.

The question vibrated through her being. What made him so important to her that she would risk her reputation, position, and even

---

[31] 1 Corinthians 4:9
[32] 2 Corinthians 3:2

her welfare to seek him out when the tyrannical attitudes of others were freely allowed to reign without much opposition?

She knew she had to answer the question, but not for the sake of those around her, but for her own benefit.

The Dawning of a New Day

Love is a learned virtue. It serves as the heart, soul, motivation, and inspiration for the Christian life. Love is also the great test of every Christian as to the validity of his or her salvation, attitude, and testimony. Jesus stated that the world would know we are His followers, because of our love for one another. At the heart of this is the desire to do right by others, show forgiveness towards unspeakable offenses, pray for our enemy, do good to those who hate and use us, and to bring a real contrast to others as to the wonder of God's incredible love.[33]

During my spiritual journey, the question would arise, what is the purpose behind the events of my life? The question would take me back to the reality that I was being prepared to meet Jesus, to see Jesus, and to tell others of Jesus. Every bend in the road was an opportunity to experience a new adventure with Him, every valley a time of humiliation and personal growth, every canyon the enlargement of character, and every mountain a time of endurance and revelation.

Hindsight showed me it was about enriching my testimony about Jesus, and when people asked what made my life different in trying times, what gave me hope in a dark world, what became my answer during senseless times, and what kept my heart from fainting in times of overwhelming loss, my answer would be simple and pure: Jesus of Nazareth, the Son of the Living God. But, how do you describe or explain Jesus? You can't unless it is from the premise of godly love that utterly consumes your heart with the reality of who He is.[34] I realized that I would be spending my time on earth answering this question from different angles, premises, and experiences.

---

[33] Matthew 5:10-12, 43-45; John 13:34,35
[34] Romans 5:1-5

When we start out on our journey of life to experience this phenomenon called love, we begin from the premise of worldly presentations, self-serving examples, and fleshly expectations. We learn in time that self-serving love can become stagnant and cruelly indifferent, fleshly love fickle, conditional, and judgmental, and worldly love unrealistic and disappointing.

As people pursue love from these different earth-based perspectives, worldly love leaves them disillusioned, fleshly love leaves them unsatisfied and angry, and self-serving love becomes an insatiable appetite that drives them to ever satisfy it to keep its driving torments at bay. The problem is that when love fails people from any of these perspectives, they not only mock such love, but they become skeptical towards the concept of love. They can't envision it being real; thereby, they often reject the moral fiber of it as they chase after lusts, or type of lifestyle that will make them "happy."

As Christians we find ourselves in a great struggle about the matter of love because we begin with the self-serving, fleshly and worldly premise of what we understand about it, and try to institute the Christian life into our ideas about love, without realizing we are perverting what constitutes godly love.

We might sense that the premise of godly love begins with the example of the sacrificial act of Christ on the cross, but since there has been no personal denial of self, Christ's sacrifice is often embraced at the point of self-serving love. After all, the cross of Christ is all about ME, esteeming the value of ME, Christ dying for ME, and who in their right mind would die for trash? When ME is the premise and emphasis in the Christian walk, we will adjust the Christian life to fit that very narrative. We haven't realized that Christ may not have died for trash, but He did die on behalf of those who were enemies of God and His truth.[35]

Without self-denial we graduate to the perspective of fleshly love. In fleshly love there is a give and take to make sure one's importance is established and needs are met in the relationship. There are methods of manipulation to employ and emotional games to develop in order to

---

[35] Romans 5:6-8; James 4:4; 1 John 4:4

ensure we experience the world's presentation of love as a means to secure personal satisfaction and happiness.

By instituting the love of the world into our Christianity, we end up with a Christian life that has no "teeth," lacks heart, and becomes self-serving. Without godly love, Christianity becomes a religion of do's and don'ts, which eventually becomes judgmental towards the Lord's way of doing something. It quickly becomes frustrated and angry that God's love actually turns out to be foreign to us, and that we can't control Him by playing on emotions to get our way.

Hindsight began to show me that the journey entailed a process that allowed me to learn what real love both looked like and acted. However, the process was long and tedious because in our limited understanding we do not always know what we are looking for when we encounter darkness descending upon our soul about spiritual truths.

The darkness was sometimes great upon my soul. Some people call it, "the dark night of the soul" where nothing makes sense. At such times it seems as if God is being unfair or, perhaps He is not hearing you in your plight. You want to shake off the numbness that is threatening to engulf you in what seems like a dark grave that is nothing more than an entrance into an abyss of nothingness. The darkness is like a heavy blanket on you, while what resembles graveclothes fearfully tighten around you, stifling your breathing, and causing the indifference of coldness to settle on your resolve, while a shroud of hopelessness enfolds you.

I was wrestling at different times with why the way was so hard and seemed so long.[36] I wanted to seek perspective from others, but I had learned that at such times people can take on a pose of judgmentalism born out of ignorance instead of true ministry. Even though I had a few friends around me that knew my inner challenge was great, I sensed that this was my course that I had to personally walk out until the light began to dawn on the dark, cold terrain.

It is hard to count the wrestling matches one has before the Lord.[37] There are many headstones marking graves that I encountered along

---

[36] Numbers 21:4
[37] Acts 14:22; Galatians 5:16-18; Jude 3

the way in my spiritual wildernesses with my name engraved on them. The first grave was marked, "Rayola's sins," the second "Rayola's best," the third "Rayola's pseudo faiths," followed by "Rayola's pride," and "Rayola's strength" and so on. There were many headstones, but they usually had one of the main themes previously mentioned engraved on them as to what they represented. The Lord used different instruments to deal with each area. The cross of Christ was used in relationship to sins, brokenness when it came to my best, testing to expose my waning faith, failures to humble me at the point of my pride, and physical sickness to reveal the fickleness of my strength.

The more I came face-to-face with myself, the more inept, pathetic, and small I felt. At one point my ineptness became my focal point. I hit a wall of utter hopelessness as I could not figure out how to overcome or change it. After wrestling with it for a couple of days the Lord penetrated the darkness with a simple impression, "Focus on Me."

It was clear I was experiencing different aspects of my relationship with the Lord. He was to be my all and all, but in order to take His rightful place in my life, the characteristics associated with the "old man" had to be identified, confronted, and mortified every time they managed to raise their head.[38]

Once the light highlighted my ineptness, the only thing that brought comfort to my tormented, weary soul was to turn my eyes on Jesus. Each time I came face to face with my smallness and looked up, the greater Jesus became to me. It was then that I realized that the walk through the wilderness of the world was for the sole purpose of shedding the "old man" so that the "new man" could be erected in my life and exalted in preparation for the glory to come.

The "new man" was the life of Jesus Christ in me. The New Testament epistles are full of what it means for a believer to have their life **in Christ** and what it means for Christ to be **in the believer**. The biggest problem Christians have in their Christian walk is that they make Christ too small as they exalt their responsibility to somehow establish some "religious life" and "personal righteousness."

---

[38] Colossians 3:5-11

The word "in" in this sense is all inclusive. In other words, you can't add to what we as believers have in Christ nor can anyone take away from who He is in us. The more I considered who I was in Christ, the more His life in me became a reality, and the more I realized that Christ was in me, the more I began to understand I was to live His life, not mine.[39]

It became obvious that the "new life" in me began to define who I was in light of eternity. The more the light of Christ was illuminated to me, the more I began to see who He was. Intellectually I knew who He was, but the one truth that continued to be confirmed to me was that intellectual knowledge is only one-dimensional. Jesus Christ who is eternal is far from being one dimensional and to keep Him in that limited sphere is to keep Him trapped in the shadows of concepts, kept undefined by mere outlines, perplexing by shades of grey that represent abstracts and unrealistic standards, and rendered colorless by lifeless ideas. He is often caged by theology, made to appear as being hypocritical by man's traditions, and controllable by religious presentations.

My experiences and encounters with the Lord challenged every bit of what I thought I initially understood about Him, as well as turned upside down what I assumed I knew, and caused all my presumptions about Him to be turned inside out, to only be taken up in a whirlwind of judgment that cast it to the far corners of the universe. Many times I stood empty handed when it came to the religious notions I so valued and trusted in my first years as a Christian. As I struggled with the vanity of such notions, I was reminded that the tangible will always dissipate in my hands, but in doing so, it allowed me the small window of opportunity to grab a hold of the intangible, the unseen, the eternal Rock of Heaven.[40]

My journey has taught me many important lessons. Some lessons were new, but many reaffirmed what I had already learned in the past. As I meditated on the lessons I learned, I realized that each experience brought me to the same place. Whether it was a lesson about my faith

---

[39] Galatians 2:20; Colossians 3:4
[40] 2 Corinthians 4:15-18

to trust God and let Him be God, or the one that brought me back to the cross of Christ, reminding me of humble beginnings, forgiveness, reconciliation, and restoration, or the necessity of daily applying my personal cross to gain Him, or to remember all strength comes from God and is found in personal weakness, every lesson brought me to my awareness of my need to see Jesus in the midst of it.[41]

Each step of the way worked some purity in me so I would be brought to my personal Mount of Transfiguration where my limited understanding parted so I could see more of His glory. As Paul reminded me, I am to be brought from glory to glory.[42]

I marveled how the Lord faithfully brought me each step of the way. He started as my Savior, still hidden in shadows, but the more I experienced Him in the different and challenging places in my life the more the glorious light of His life disbursed the shadows, adding details to His character, bringing His ways into clarity, and adding colorful dimension to His teachings and instructions. The more Jesus became a reality to me, the more my heart attitude changed towards Him.

I had to clearly seek Jesus in every challenge, at every bend, and in every circumstance to gain His heavenly perspective. Each new revelation of Him caused my love to grow for Him, enlarged my faith, and inspired me to come higher regardless of the challenging terrain. As His sheep I became hungrier and thirstier for the paths of righteousness that would lead me to the pastures of His abiding care and will, to experience real rest in Him.[43]

I can't tell you how precious He became to me during some of my most trying times. Appreciation rose up in me when I pondered His salvation during the darkest of times, while finding hope in His love and comfort in His faithfulness, but each realization of His greatness revealed there was so much more to Him. No one word could describe Him, and titles didn't stand on their own without definition, and descriptions fell short of hitting the mark as to explaining Him. He was and continues to be the faithful friend who would never let me down, the

---

[41] Philippians 3:7-10
[42] Matthew 17:1-9; 2 Corinthians 3:18
[43] Psalm 23:3; Matthew 5:6; 11:28-30

lover of my soul who would challenge me to be the best I could be, a fair, caring Lord in an incredible household, and a just king over an unseen kingdom. His right arm always empowered me and His left arm continued to help me up in trying times, and both are ever capable of reaching great heights as well as into the depths of hell, if necessary, to pick me up. His eyes penetrated my soul with concern and His countenance radiated in such a way that it always led me to Him. His broad shoulders carry the burdens of the world, His words of truth stop and silence the enemy, and His hand continues to touch every aspect of my soul with healing. He is wonderful in every way, the capable counsellor who brings wisdom to all matters, proves to be the Almighty in all of His ways and interventions, always a committed family member that ever speaks of the Father's love and commitment to save me and make me whole, and upon seeking Him, would ultimately bring peace to my heart.[44]

My understanding of Him would also grow as I sought to see Him through the eyes of others. To Abraham, He was the ram who replaced his son, Isaac on Mount Moriah, while to Jacob He stood atop a ladder that connected heaven with earth. Moses experienced His glory from the top of a rock, hid in the cleft of it, and the elders of Israel witnessed His heavenly transparency as He walked atop a paved road of sapphire at Mount Sinai. Joshua took his shoes off and bowed before Him when he encountered Him as the Captain of the host of heaven. The Apostle Peter identified Him as chief Shepherd who will appear, the Apostle Paul spoke of Him as being the unspeakable gift from heaven, Jude made reference to Him as the only wise God, our Savior, and the Apostle John after Jesus introduced Himself as the Alpha and Omega, the beginning and the ending, fainted before Him as the great Judge. The Lord laid His hand on him saying, "Fear not; I am the first and the last: I am he that liveth, and was dead; and behold, I am alive for evermore, Amen; and have the keys of hell and of death."[45]

---

[44] Psalm 89:13,14; 98:1; Isaiah 9:6, 7; 59:1; Luke 4:18; John 18:36; Hebrews 3:2-6; Revelation 1:8

[45] Genesis 22:7,8,13,14; 28:12,13; Exodus 24:10,11; 33:21-23; Joshua 5:13-15; 2 Corinthians 9:15; 1 Peter 5:4; Jude 25; Revelation 1:8, 11,17, 18

To see Jesus became my heart cry. At times I was overwhelmed, while many times I felt undone and unworthy to even catch glimpses of Him. In my weakness He became my strength and in darkness, I discovered His grace was sufficient.[46] The more real He became to me the more my love became defined by who He was. The more my love for Him matured, the more it caused Him to be magnified in my eyes and the greater my worship became towards Him.

It was clear that as my mind was enlarged to embrace greater aspects of Jesus, my sacrifice of praise could rise higher into the heavens allowing me to soar in the midst of eternal possibilities while exploring aspects of His glory that was clearly defining my worship and service to Him.[47]

It is only as I discovered who I was in Jesus that I became aware of my authority in Him and the inheritance that awaited me. The more I exposed myself to Him the more I took on His attitude about matters and the greater I took on His likeness as a child of God reflecting His glory.

Each new revelation of Jesus was like the morning star rising on the terrain of my soul, creating the dawning of a new day in my Christian walk. It became clear that the deeper He went in me, the higher I came in Him. The greater the affliction, the greater the deliverance, the more the challenge the more character was forged in me, and the greater the suffering was within me the greater the identification I had in Him.[48]

Sometimes, when I went to describe what was happening to me, I couldn't always find the right words and I wasn't sure that anyone would understand. I even sensed I had to guard some of it because it could be defiled by those who would never understand the deep places that the Lord had led me to cause me to become pliable in His hands so I would be quick to rise up at His invitation in order to learn to follow Him into an abundant life. I had to keep my ears tuned for Him so that when those brief moments came of Him knocking on my door, seeking fellowship,

---

[46] 2 Corinthians 12:8-10
[47] John 4:22-24; Hebrews 13:15-16
[48] Roman 8:17; 2 Timothy 2:12

they would not elude me. I had to be prepared to step into the unknown in order to learn to soar in the heavenlies.[49]

It was obvious as I came to places of fellowship with the Lord that my love for Him was being transformed; thereby, my mind was being changed, my heart more pliable in the hands of the great husbandman to bring forth the precious spices of our relationship, and my life a consecrated, living sacrifice ready to be offered up for His glory.

As my love grew and became transformed, I knew there was always more. Love is eternal. There is no place to mark its beginning and there will be no end to it. Transforming love had enriched the spices in the garden of my heart with sweet fellowship with my Lord, and it had caused me to soar in heavenly possibilities but I knew that transforming love was another stepping stone, and that beyond it was the immeasurable, the indescribable, and the eternal.

The Chiefest Among Ten Thousand

The handmaidens' question about what was so special about the Shulamite girl's beloved that she would even charge them to watch for him, caused her to connect her desperation with what was becoming obvious to her—that she so loved her beloved, so cherished him, and so needed him to be her breath, her inspiration, her very life.

She sighed at her ability to so soon forget how wonderful it was to fellowship with him, as well as spend time with him in the inner chambers of growth, and walk with him in the garden of communion. How could she become complacent towards him at such a time of his visitation, dismissive towards his desire to come in out of the night into the light of the sweet warmth of love and the comfort of her presence.

The Shulamite girl may have committed an insignificant offense towards her beloved in the eyes of others, but her heart told her that her complacency was a terrible affront against their relationship, against his love for her. She couldn't let her personal, worldly comforts come

---

[49] John 10:10; Revelation 3:20

between them again. She must find him, she must right the terrible wrong she committed.

Meanwhile, the handmaidens of Jerusalem were waiting for her answer. What made her beloved so special, so unique that she would charge them to find him? What features or characteristic would stand out that would cause them to identify him if they encountered him?[50]

The first thing she had to note about him was his godliness. There was nothing impure in His ways, inconsistent in His speech, tainted about his motives, or questionable about his character. He had a complexion that revealed he lived a healthy lifestyle that was clean and vibrant. There was nothing sluggish in his walk, and his strength was at its height, allowing him to accomplish what was within his heart to do. Clearly, these characteristics made him stand out above others. In fact, she could rightly say that he was the chiefest among 10,000.

Her description made her realize why her heart had become so desperate for him. There was no one like him, and among the men around her he clearly stood out. She had just begun to describe him, and as each point of description came forth, she realized that it backed up and verified her claims about him being the chiefest among thousands.

As she described his head, she recognized that he held a predominate place, not only in her life, but among those who knew and loved him. He not only stood tall and distinguished among the thousands but he was a natural leader whose leadership and example revealed that he possessed divine attributes, capable of reflecting the life and glory from above. His black hair spoke of his vigor and power to bring about the tasks before him, whether as king over his people or as a shepherd leading his people.

His eyes spoke volumes that was veiled to others, but not to her. Her times of fellowship with him had allowed her to look into his eyes to catch glimpses of heavenly mysteries being unveiled that had been first immersed in living waters of God's Spirit and washed with the pure milk of truth. His eyes were fitly set on her, ever looking into her soul,

[50] You can scripturally follow the description of the beloved in Song of Solomon 5:10-16

preparing to respond to her heart cries, as well as the slightest of gestures, and the simplest of invitations.

There were his cheeks! How many times had he turned his cheek to her, for her to lightly touch as a sign of tenderness that brought sweetness to their times together, or to kiss it as a greeting that spoke of expectation and excitement of the fellowship that awaited. As she thought of the preciousness of his cheeks, she realized that they could be slapped and bruised as a means to thrust personal insult or rejection of him as a person. Such a thought tore at her heart, causing her to wonder if her inaction towards him was like slamming the door in his face, bruising his cheeks.

His lips reminded her of kingly authority and glory. She was aware that Yahweh clothed the world with the beauty of flowers, the uniqueness of His creatures, and the glory of the firmament. Man may do his best to sew together the finest of materials, but the real glory of something can only be brought out by the Creator.[51] The Shulamite girl had concluded that it was simplicity that distinguished beauty, the design and function highlighted the uniqueness of Yahweh's creatures, and the vastness emphasized His endless glory. She was aware that her beloved was called and ordained as king, and Yahweh was confirming it by arraying his lips with heavenly spices of truth and nuggets of wisdom that would speak of heavenly glory from above.

His hands reminded her of gentleness and strength. His gentle touch brought calmness to her soul and their strength reminded her of meekness that spoke of regimentation in light of his activities. He never stepped outside of what was required and necessary, and according to plan. Clearly, the gold rings reminded her of the many facets of His unending love towards her, a love that was divine and eternal.

The gold rings were set in beryl. This helped her to recognize the key to the presence of meekness in his activities, and the only way to describe the transparency produced by his meekness was to relate it to beryl. Beryl can prove to vary in color but never in its transparency. It will never betray what it is and what it is to highlight. It was clear that his works were firmly established and always brought to completion.

---

[51] Matthew 6:28-30

The Shulamite girl realized that the strength of his hands found its source in his inward character. His inner character reminded her of prized ivory that pointed to the pain and sacrifice of a life. She realized that he had put great value on his love for her, even though her responses at times had cost him mental anguish and caused emotional pain.

His character was enhanced by a love that was not surface, while it served as an expression of his inner quality. It was clear that this love was not only an intricate part of his character but it was overlaid by the transparency of heavenly sustenance and assurance.

The other aspect of his character was that it enabled him to have right standing before heaven and man, bringing her much stability. He could not be moved from what was righteous, knocked off of what was honorable, or ever be persuaded to move from what was just. He was like an immovable rock, a sure foundation, a cornerstone firmly planted on and within the eternal plan of Yahweh.

There was also the uniqueness of his countenance. Oh, how it revealed the excellence of his character that stood tall like the cedars of Lebanon, reaching far beyond what was considered to be the best of the present world, as to touch the unspeakable glory of heaven.

The fruit of his mouth had proved to be sweet to her. His words edified her spirit, enlarged her mind, and brought satisfaction to her soul. He never spoke out of turn, impulsively made empty claims, or defrauded himself with false impressions or promises. She could hold his words close to her heart as they served as an anchor of hope and joy to her soul. At times, His wise words lifted her up in glorious inspiration to experience heights that became too glorious for her to describe.

As she came to the end of describing him, there was only one statement that could define him, "he is altogether lovely." [52] It was the only word that could emphasize the delight he brought to her life because of the strong affections she had for him, the longing desire to be in his presence, his goodly countenance that could comfort as well

---

[52] Song of Solomon 5:16

as penetrate her very being with warmth, and the fellowship that proved pleasant and satisfying.

At that moment she realized something else of significance. She started out simply being invited to his table, ending up in his chambers, graduating to being elevated as his betrothed, and becoming part of his inheritance as his sister, but now she realized he was also her friend.[53]

What an incredible discovery. After all, did not Yahweh call Abraham friend because of his faith towards Him? Love and faith walk hand in hand.[54] Love is the motive behind the "why's" but faith is the inspiration behind actions of faithfulness that is ever bore upon the wings of heavenly love.

Her journey with her beloved revealed that love starts out in the emotional realm of affections that are often based on self-serving imaginations, which then slides into fleshly desires, skips over uncertainties, faces obstacles, grows in character, and at its height can become complacent while sitting on the laurels of past assumptions and resting on presumptuous expectations.

Her great heights had also set her up for her great failure to respond, but she began to realize that in the process, her love for her beloved was being transformed. This became clearer to her as the young handmaidens of the city asked her upon addressing her as the "fairest among women," where had her beloved gone, where had he turned aside and where could they personally seek him.[55]

These young maidens had recognized her incredible beauty and perhaps realized that the inner glow was because of her love for her beloved. The Shulamite girl knew one can't influence the attitudes and affections of others towards a stranger unless his or her attitude and affections are real because they have truly been captured. It was obvious these young handmaidens wanted to search him out for themselves to see if he was all she had declared him to be.[56]

---

[53] Ibid
[54] Isaiah 41:8; Galatians 5:5,6
[55] Song of Solomon 6:1
[56] Ibid

It suddenly dawned on the Shulamite girl where her beloved would be—in the garden where they had shared such sweet fellowship in the past.[57] It would only make sense that he would go there and wait for her. It was clear by the unfolding of her love for him in her description of him that it had gone beyond girlish affections to a transformed love that would produce another type of intimacy. They clearly belonged to each other and she knew by his character that he was not the type to hide from her in unknown places so that he couldn't be found, nor would he throw his hands up in the air in utter disgust and despair and walk away from her for good.[58] It is true he had caused her to rise up and seek him, but he knew that once the timing was right and the confusion of desperation parted that she would remember their precious place of fellowship, a place that was personal and couldn't be shared with others.

Her experience with her beloved had taught her that the higher she came in her love and understanding of him, the more she was elevated in her position with him. This preeminent place was only seen by him, but he was the only one who counted. The opinions of others were clearly becoming less and less important to her. What mattered is what he thought about her, and that could only be expressed when the two were alone. She knew it would be from that elevated place that he would describe the transformation that had occurred in her life because of her love for him.

True to his ways, she found him in his garden, and true to his past responses to her, he described her.[59] His first description of her was that she was beautiful, but his comparison of her beauty was to Tirzah, Jerusalem, and a dreadful army. Tirzah meant "delightful."[60] There was the youngest daughter of Zelophehad ,who along with her four sisters had claimed their inheritance in the Promised Land because there was no male heir.[61] These series of events revealed that the inheritance belonged to the women who were descendants of Abraham as well.

---

[57] Song of Solomon 6:2

[58] Song of Solomon 6:3

[59] The description of the Shulamite girl can be scripturally followed in Song of Solomon 6:4-10

[60] Smith's Bible Dictionary

[61] Numbers 26:33; 27:1-11

There was also a place of Tirzah that served as a residence of kings. It was clear that her love for him had made her more of a delight to him, pointing to the great inheritance that was attached to it, and that he no longer considered it to be common, but it was now dressed in royal garb.

She knew that Jerusalem was Yahweh's chosen city, but it was preferred because of the witness of the tabernacle in its midst. It was clear that her beloved had chosen her, but now her love for him was preferred because it had a standing witness that it operated in the spiritual realm and reached upward beyond the normal to embrace the extraordinary.

As she looked back, she was reminded of the many great battles that had occurred in relationship to the love she now possessed. There were many due to the different things that tried to take her affections captive. At times the battle appeared to start out as a simple tug of war with her attractions and affections, but each time it would slide into a great battle. The battles often proved dreadful because she fell short of being victorious in so many of them. However, she had to note in his description that the army was not lifting up weapons but banners. The banners revealed that victory had indeed been secured and now the spoils of the battle could be enjoyed.

He then spoke of her eyes. Many times, she had seen the strength and steadiness of his love for her in his eyes, but now he made reference that her love was not only singular towards him, but now it was strong and steady, and it was overwhelming to him to see the depth of her love for him.

The mention of her hair spoke of her pure devotion of love to him. It was no longer just a matter of fickle sentiment, fleeing emotions, conditional, and self-serving notions, but it spoke of a love that was consecrated. It was now a standing vow that would not be moved away from its commitment and responsibility. It was a love that would never falter again or be unresponsive.

She could now properly process her responsibilities towards him, which would prove to be fruitful and beneficial to their relationship. It was true that the depth of it was hidden from the world and the immature, but the world could not understand it and the immature were not prepared to tread into its depth. What she knew by his words was that this

155

transforming love would make their fellowship together richer and sweeter.

She understood that her beloved had such love that as king he could embrace every loyal subject of his kingdom and as shepherd, he could care for every wandering sheep he came upon. Even though his love could embrace that which was royal, elevate those who were common, and take under his wing the pure, poor, and vulnerable, he would not share their love with another. His affections could not be seduced by the power or greed of royalty, his emotions taken on a fruitless ride, and his sentiment twisted into misguided sympathy.

He confirmed this unspoken reality by calling her his undefiled dove that stood uniquely alone in every way. As undefiled, she stood pure, clean before him and as a dove, he recognized her devotion was singular towards him. He acknowledged she was chosen in her mother's womb for her position and placed in his life. She had received a special blessing, and as a result she stood out even among the royal members of the court. There was no doubt that she was a product of grace that had been bestowed on her by love.

It was true that at times the law of Moses could overshadow God's grace with its various requirements and activities, but she was aware that the law could not earn her any status before Yahweh. The more she had tried to become justified by the law the more she became undone by it. It became clear why Abraham, who was before Moses, was justified by faith and not the Law.[62] Faith was a grace that Yahweh imparts into open hearts, and it was becoming clear that He had imparted it into her heart and that others, regardless of status and personal attitudes towards her, recognized that such grace was present in her life.

Her beloved's description continued to reveal the place she held in his heart. He had long ago seen her potential and had lovingly invested in their relationship according to the heights she could reach as a person. With his description of her, she was beginning to see herself through his eyes and it was exciting, but humbling.

---

[62] Romans 3:19,20; 4:3

In one statement, he seemed to summarize how he viewed her with a question, "Who is she that looketh forth as the morning, fair as the moon, clear as the sun, and terrible as an army with banners?"[63] The question highlighted her in a certain way, but did she really fit the description?

The handmaidens had asked her what made her beloved distinct, but now he was bringing distinction to her, highlighting the life that was now developed in her. Life represents the light of the soul, and regardless of how intense the darkness might be, the light will always penetrate the darkness to reveal the dawning of a new day.[64] The mention of the moon being fair implied that the life in her cast a certain beauty on the terrain, even when the night was casting immense shadows and that in the daytime the light of her life brought clarity to the beauty that existed in her soul. The mention of the armies reminded her that there had been many battles taking place in her soul as to who would influence and dominate her affections, but the banners declared that she had experienced great victories in that particular area.

His final description had caused her to suddenly feel overwhelmed. She found herself on unsure footing about how to respond and act. She had actually become embarrassed by his accolades. It was clear to her that he was speaking out of love, but the memory of her inaction towards him was still very much skirting in and out of the outer fringes of her mind. She knew he was sincere, but she was not sure she was at the place where she could accept his evaluation.

She had to rein in her uncomfortable feelings and get her bearings. She went to the garden where she could examine and break through the exterior of her feelings in order to come to terms with what was real. She wanted to get down to the meat of her own character to see if what he said was really being reflected through her life. She had to check out the fruit of her life. After all, she was a mere branch in the scheme of things and the fruit of her life would reveal if she was thoroughly

---

[63] Song of Solomon 6:10
[64] Matthew 6:22,23; John 1:4,5

connected to the true vine.[65] She could not settle on the laurels of wishful thinking while flying high on what could turn out to be mere flattery. She had to know for herself if she was worthy of such praise.

As she meditated on the matter, she was suddenly enraptured by a simple truth, and that is if he saw such things in her they must be so. He would never flatter her in order to seduce her into a false narrative or a compromising situation. She could trust that what he was seeing was true. Granted, she knew there were inconsistencies in her character, but she had to be willing to accept his evaluation if she was to be set free to reach her potential and finally come to maturity in her relationship with him.[66]

There was no reason for her to hold back. She was free to quickly claim her place beside him. He had placed her there and his love for her had taken her hand and prepared the way for her to enter into more intimate places, but now it was time for her to rise up and take the initiative to invite and take his hand.

Her thoughts were interrupted. At first, she heard what she thought to be the wind gently rustling through the limbs of the trees, but as she listened it sounded like an echo. Eventually the cadence of the echo began to converge together into the voices of young women, and they were calling out to her, "Return, return, O Shulamite; return, return, that we may look upon thee. What will ye see in the Shulamite? As it were the company of two armies?"[67]

Initially she was puzzled. Why would these young women send forth such an invitation to her; and then she remembered. After she had described her beloved, they wanted to see if her description was true, and now that her beloved described her, these young handmaidens wanted to see if his description was correct. It made sense that since they were trying to find their place in the religious culture and practices that they were seeking examples in which they could imitate. Her beloved had arrayed her with such beauty and graces in his description

---

[65] Song of Solomon 6:11; Matthew 7:16; John 15:1-8; 1 Corinthians 11:28; 2 Corinthians 13:5
[66] According to Smith's Bible Dictionary, Amminadib in Song of Solomon 6:12, means "willing people."
[67] Song of Solomon 6:13

of her that they were now curious about her, attracted to those qualities that made her distinct and had caused her to be preferred by the king.

What was interesting is that they made reference to two armies. She remembered what happened with Jacob where he witnessed God's host and he called the place "Mahanaim."[68] "Mahanaim" signifies two hosts or two camps.[69] There were various armies of earth seen of men, and then there were the unseen hosts and camps that are ever present with God's people. Jacob realized he had encountered the unseen host and the great prophet Elisha asked Yahweh to reveal the invisible horses and the chariots of fire that surrounded him.[70]

The Shulamite girl knew her identity with the king gave her a certain protection, but it appeared that she also had the protection of the unseen host. This did not surprise her because one of the Psalms declares, "For he shall give his angels charge over thee, to keep thee in all thy ways."[71] However, the fact that the handmaidens recognized that these two camps surrounded her made her wonder if their eyes had somewhat been opened to see into the unseen realm of demons and angels.

The Unspeakable Gift
(The Second Companion)

The former slave girl struggled with the best way to answer the question of the onlookers. It was clear by her appearance that she was a spectacle to those looking upon her, and she had no semblance that would identify her to her Lord's household and kingdom. Her first encounter with her Lord was when he purchased her and saved her from the auction block. In a sense, she had been on an auction block ever since her birth. It was clear from her present situation that she must not forget her humble beginnings because she was born into slavery.[72]

---

[68] Genesis 32:2
[69] Smith's Bible Dictionary.
[70] 2 Kings 6:11-19
[71] Psalm 91:11
[72] Zechariah 4:10

Her parents were slaves, her household was ruled by harsh taskmasters, and her life was held in the grip of oppression. Before she was purchased, she had resolved that slavery and oppression would be her lot in life, but because of this man stepping on the scene and inserting himself into her plight, she now had hope.

She looked at the inquisitive onlookers. "I guess the first thing I must say is that he redeemed me from a life of utter bondage. I was on a road to nowhere, and in complete despair." She paused before continuing. "He not only redeemed me but he set me at his table. Imagine, one born in slavery sitting at the table of royalty."[73]

She almost smiled but went on, "Even though I was a slave, he offered me the finer things of life as he admitted that he was seeking a bride and he found me, chose me, and like a lost lamb led me to a safe place, a place of communion with him. He bound up my wounds and healed my emotional scars. Even though you can't tell right now, he covered my rags with white linens fit for a queen.[74]

"In my confusion he showed kindness, in my fear he showed patience, and in my pathetic state, he gave me hope." She stopped to let the information sink in, not only in their minds, but in her own heart as well.

She needed to get these truths down in her soul so that she would never forget. She continued, "In light of his goodness, I realize I'm nothing but an unattractive, normal clay jar that has benefitted daily from his personal storehouse.[75] The grace he has shown me has brought healing, the mercy he offers has brought restoration, the kindness he has provided has served as a resting place for me, and his thoughtful ways confirmed that he knew who I was and what was important to me before I did.

"I always thought material things would make a difference, but he has taught me it is the quality of my relationship, especially with him, that makes my life more valuable. I always felt that riches were based on such things as gold, silver, and priceless gems, but he has taught me

---

[73] Luke 9:56; Roman 6:20; 7:14; Ephesians 1:7; 1 Timothy 2:6
[74] Psalm 147:3; Isaiah 61:1-3; Luke 4:18; Revelation 19:7,8
[75] 2 Corinthians 4:7

that he is the real prize that adds value and meaning to my life. In light of him, all the world can offer is nothing but dung and will prove so when he is not present to fill one's life with his love, joy, and peace."

She paused as she became overwhelmed by her own description of him. How could she let him go back into the night without tending to his needs and seeking out fellowship with him, regardless of the time it might have taken. Was he not worth it? It was then her heart became overwhelmed, but the expressions of the onlookers told her they wanted to hear more and know more about her Lord.

She decided to be honest with them. "You have to excuse me as I feel a bit overwhelmed. I didn't realize until now how much my Lord owns my heart. I always knew I held his heart, but I never realized until now that he has taken possession of my heart as well.

"When he met me, I had a broken heart, and it was at his table that my heart was made new, and it was at his feet that he threw his garment over me to show his intention of making me his bride, causing such hope and peace to flood my heart. I can't tell you how many times in our communion together that my heart burned within me towards him, while my spirit was quickened by his words as my joy was made complete.[76]

"It is because of him I have a future, an inheritance. I'm not only a part of his household, but part of his family. I not only sit at his table, but I also hold a seat of prominence with him. I have his ear which gives me authority to make a difference in the kingdom. Granted, I have failed to understand my position at times, but I know that I am seated in high places with him.[77]

"He alone has given me identity because, as you see, it is tied into my relationship with him. The watchmen of the city and the gatekeeper assumed by my dress that I no longer have a viable relationship with my Lord, but I do. He didn't kick me out of his household; rather, I failed to meet with him when he came to my door and now, I'm looking for him."

She shook her head in disbelief at her attitude and lack of actions as she continued on. "He has filled so many positions in my life. He is Lord, but he has become the lover of my soul. He is king, but he is also like a

---

[76] Ruth 3:7-14; Luke 24:32; John 6:63; 15:11
[77] Romans 8:14-17; Ephesians 2:6

protective brother that shares a common legacy. He is my master, but he has become the one who serves me in so many ways. He is my betrothed, and he has become a dear friend." [78]

As she grappled with being overwhelmed, she looked at those listening to her. She wanted to somehow articulate in one sentence what her Lord had become to her and finally the words came to her, "He is an unspeakable gift!"[79]

The realization of the revelation about her Lord that unfolded through her to the onlookers was becoming once again overwhelming to her, and almost in a whisper as if talking to herself she stated, "He keeps on giving his best, keeps on offering his all, and keeps on being faithful to me when I am being fickle and untrustworthy towards him."

Her voice grew stronger in her description of him as she continued, "He is the rock that never moves, the cornerstone that is sure, and fortress that hides me.[80]

"Oh, how I need to see him and to seek his forgiveness for being complacent towards his call. I knew it was his voice, but I was late in responding and now in the night I realize how valuable his love is to me, how undone and miserable I am without him."

As the last three words came out of her mouth, she was reminded of something she had forgotten in her confusion and desperation. There was one place her Lord would be waiting for her and that was in the garden.

Without any further words, she immediately ran in the direction of the garden, unaware that the onlookers were following her. After all, she was not running towards the garden to lead them; rather, she was running toward the garden to find her Lord for herself.

To her relief, he was waiting there for her. She ran and flung herself into his waiting arms. Through her sobs she asked forgiveness, and clung to him with all her might. She remembered that the last time she had to search for him, she felt she would never let go of him when she

---

[78] John 15:14-16
[79] 2 Corinthians 9:15
[80] Psalm 18:2; Romans 9:33; 1 Peter 2:6-8

found him, but in the latest situation she had let him slip through her fingers because she wasn't prepared to meet him in a greater way.

If only her selfishness would cease to be and her self-centeredness would take flight, she would not have failed her Lord, but it was there ready to rise up in protest when matters didn't prove convenient or comfortable. She had to face the fact that her selfishness would reign if she gave way to its rights, logic, or excuses.

Her Lord lifted her face so he could look into her eyes. She wondered what he could see through her tears. She felt shame peek around the corners of her emotions, but she knew her meeting with him was not about her shame, but about forgiveness and restoration.

He smiled at her. It was then that his eyes mirrored what he was seeing. In his eyes, she could see a beautiful bouquet reflecting back at her. There was a red rose pointing to love, a white lily that spoke of purity, a yellow daffodil that pointed to joy and flowers that were made of five pedals that reminded her that all work was a matter of grace. There was greenery that pointed to fruitfulness and flowers that spoke of friendship and others of fragrance. There was such an abundance of life represented in that bouquet that she could barely take it all in.

She knew he was simply reflecting the work that had been done in her soul by him, a work she hadn't realized existed until now. The revelation brought restoration, but it unnerved her at the same time. She felt almost embarrassed by it because she was fully aware of her many failures. However, the moment was not about her failures but his work in her life, heart, and upon her mind. It was not about her defeats, but what He had managed to do in her to bring forth victory. It was clear that her life was not to speak of herself, but it was to reflect him and his good work on her behalf and in her.

She found herself being humbled by the experience. She slowly mouthed the two words that had clearly formed on her lips, "THANK YOU." She realized her latest inaction had broken her, but when she found him, the broken pieces had been miraculously placed into a mosaic that her Lord prized and was ready to display to others.

She excused herself to get her bearings. The revelation that she had received was strange to her. Yes, she desired her life to be such a bouquet that brought honor to her Lord, but she knew her flaws: and the bouquet did not reflect any such weeds of inconsistencies.

It dawned on her that the mirror of truth kept her realistic about who she was, but her Lord's perception of her was ever calling her to choose the excellent ways so she could reach the potential of her high calling and fulfill her royal obligations at the table of service, in the harvest field of his kingdom, and in the gardens of communion.

As she was meditating on the latest revelations, she heard voices. She realized the voices came from the onlookers. They were now seeking her out. This confused her because they had followed her to her Lord, but now they sought her out.

The question, "Why," floated before her. It didn't make sense, and then she realized that the onlookers didn't have any relationship with her Lord. They were seeking her out because of her relationship to him. They wanted more and needed to be properly introduced to him, instructed in how to conduct themselves, and prepared to meet him at the point of true communion.

The former slave girl realized she now held the key that opens the door to those still enslaved to be set free. It was clear that her real work was just beginning but it was also obvious there was still much work that had to be done in her.

Coming Higher

It is easy after spending time in the valleys of humiliation, the canyons of despair, the plateaus of mediocrity, and the misty flats of confusion and compromise to desire to come higher, but it's hard to know how that will translate in your life. I always wanted to come higher, but often felt hindered by the ongoing challenges of life. I didn't realize that "higher" for a believer did not translate into some great experience or victory but in gaining the Lord's perspective about matters.

To me, I often felt like a turkey instead of an eagle. I saw myself standing on a fence but never on a high cliff. I often felt that if I took two steps forward it was only to be knocked five steps backwards. It seemed like my humanness was always tripping me up, the world was trying to pull me back to what was, and Satan was forever putting obstacles in front of me.

The battles were intense at times, but as time went on the war between the Spirit and my flesh seemed to take less time, while the attachments to the world were being torn, ripped, and purged as I encountered them; however, the battle with the unseen world seemed to escalate as the battles of the flesh and the world receded. At times I became weary with it all, but through each battle I came out with a greater understanding of the Christian life.

There were valuable lessons I learned from the ongoing battles with the three enemies of the soul. The first lesson I learned is that the great battle raging is over one's faith towards God. The flesh cried foul when things were not going right, the world enticed me to give up and give in to its false promises, and the devil tried to rob me of my faith, kill the joy of my salvation, and destroy my testimony. I learned that faith was a choice and that it was only by trusting the character of God that I could land on His promises and come to a place of rest during the battles.[81]

It was the lessons of faith that brought to focus the sovereignty of God. He was in control regardless of how out of control the world around me seemed to be. I had to trust that He was allowing certain circumstances in my life, not to destroy me, but to refine the character of my faith. The test of my character was to believe Him regardless of the giants in front of me and simply be faithful in doing right with what was before me.[82] As I took steps of obedience, the giants often disappeared, leaving me with a sense of awe.

These experiences brought me to another valuable lesson: it is what God is able to do in and through me that was the real gauge in my Christian walk and growth. In my initial years of Christianity, I made much of my Christian life about me getting it right and what I could do for God or was supposed to do when it came to my walk, but the various obstacles and hindrances eventually taught me that God was using these various means to work in me Christian virtues. He was, in reality,

---

[81] John 10:10; Galatians 5:17; Ephesians 6:10-17; Hebrews 1:6; 6:12; James 4:4; 1 John 2:15-17; Jude 3; Revelation 12:11

[82] Romans 8:28; 1 Peter 1:5-9

preparing me for what He wanted me to do, and at the right time He would bring it about.

This brought a certain liberty to me in my Christian service. I could not save anyone, change anybody's mind, or clean anyone up. Jesus was the one who died and rose again in order to save, while the Holy Spirit and the Bible are capable of convicting, transforming, and cleaning up the inner man. My responsibility was to be the voice that spoke the truth and share the Gospel, the feet that went about doing His bidding, and the hands that would reach out and touch others on His behalf.

It became obvious time and time again, if the Lord was not behind a matter it would prove to be useless in the end. If He had not ordained a matter, it was already a lost cause. In summation, what was not of God, from God, and because of God would be nothing more than vanity.[83]

I understood the emptiness of such vanity. I had spent the first years of my Christian life operating in vanity. I was doing everything in my own strength according to a lifeless religious code while falling deeper into a cesspool of compromise that ended up with me becoming a miserable, broken failure that only He could put back together.

Another lesson I had to learn was to quit looking towards the horizon for my deliverance, but instead I needed to look up for my redemption. I had learned that deliverance comes in two ways: God delivers us from something or delivers us through something. Most of us expect God to deliver us from our troubles to prove He loves us, but He loves us enough that He wants to see us mature in our life. This means delivering us through our troubles to refine our faith and bring spiritual maturity to us.[84]

Genuine faith will cause us to turn and face our troubles while trusting the Lord to deliver us through them. There are many who try to use faith like a magic wand to control circumstances instead of facing them in light of who God is. Such a practice keeps a person from ever really having to trust the Lord. It is the enlargement of our faith in the fiery trials that brings spiritual maturity to us as Christians.[85]

---

[83] Ecclesiastes 12:13,14
[84] Psalm 34:19; Luke 21:28; Acts 14:22
[85] 1 Peter 1:5-9

Enlargement of faith only comes as we learn to trust the Lord. Trusting the Lord comes down to the level of dependency one has on Him. It is hard for people to realize that some of the religious practices and methods in Christendom are to avoid giving up personal independence that sees itself as being in control; therefore, doing everything in its power to avoid becoming dependent on the one true God who can't be controlled or manipulated. It is for this reason that the preaching of the cross, whether it is Jesus' cross or our personal cross, seems foolish to the intellectual man who must control his personal understanding of events happening around him and in his world.[86]

Another important pinnacle I hit in my spiritual life was coming to terms with who I am in Christ. It is easy to become side-tracked and lose sight of what needs to be important as saints of the Most High God. In my early years as a Christian, I wrestled over what I was to do. In my faltering years of being a Christian I wrestled with what I understood, and in my growing years I wrestled with the "old man" in me to reach greater heights, but in the testing that occurred when my love was being completely transformed, I found myself wrestling with the subtle influences of the world upon my soul.

It was only as I grew in the knowledge of the Lord at each stage that I began to understand who I was in Him. It was obvious that we can't know ourselves and our potential without knowing our Creator, understanding His work as the Potter in our lives, and clearly seeing the image presented on the canvas of His Word that is to be worked into our lives by the Great Sculptor, the Holy Spirit, while pressing towards the goal to reach the place of excellency to become the finished product that would bring glory to our Creator.[87]

As I began to expose myself more to the Spirit, submit to my Lord's will, and discipline myself to walk in the godly counsel of His ways, I could sense I was being conformed to the image of my Savior and Lord. Granted, my humanness was still there, ever ready to prove how base, self-serving, and fickle it could be, but I knew there were changes

---

[86] 1 Corinthians 1:21-23
[87] Romans 8:29; 2 Corinthians 3:18; Ephesians 2:10; Philippians 3:21; 1 John 3:2

occurring in my attitude about sin, as well as in regards to priorities and importance in light of the heart of God.

This change was also confirmed in other ways. Other believers became attracted to what I possessed. They were drawn by the wisdom of it, sometimes challenged by the touch of eternity upon it, and became hungry to possess it themselves. They wanted to come to the same well I had been drinking from to partake of the living and refreshing waters that brought me joy, satisfaction, and at times sobriety. They knew it was not me but Jesus in me. They knew that I didn't possess anything apart from what was being established in me through the Holy Spirit. They knew it was Jesus, but they came seeking the right keys, tools, or revelations that would give them the means to tap into the well for themselves so that it would become a fountain where the water would freely flow through their lives.[88]

The biggest change I could see came in service. In the beginning, it was the Lord who invited me to come to His table, and as the Great Shepherd, He pursued me during my independent wanderings, while as the Loving Lord and parent, He contended with me in my rebellion. He sometimes quietly listened to my excuses, my complaints, and my reasoning to only speak those things that brought humility and perspective. He knew when to back off to force me to decide if He was worth it to me to step past myself and my self-serving ways to seek Him out when I realized that life didn't make sense, unless He was the center of it.

However, the time arrived when I knew it was up to me to reach out to Him, invite Him to be part of my journey, to walk with me through the terrain, and to share my adventures with me. We must remember that as believers we are strangers in this world, and as pilgrims the world is not our real home, but in our journey, we are carrying seeds of eternal life in the form of a valuable message called the Gospel.[89]

As His servants, we must be about His business in advancing the cause of His household, as His soldiers we must be prepared to march to fight for our Lord's unseen kingdom, and as His ambassadors we

---

[88] Isaiah 12:3; John 7:37-39; Ephesians 1:17, 18
[89] Mark 16:15,16; Romans 1:16; 1 Corinthians 2:2; 9:16; 1 Peter 2:11

must be ready to travel wherever we are sent to promote the goodwill of His kingdom to those seeking refuge for their souls. Granted, like Moses, we must not go unless He is with us, we must not venture unless first instructed to do so, and we must not assume a matter unless He confirms it by opening the doors, and even though it is in service to Him, we must recognize that we need to always first invite Him to walk beside us, to guide us through the terrain, and to be the source behind all we do on His behalf. [90]

I had to ever seek Him before I made any moves in ministry. I didn't have a personal life apart from Him because He is my life. I had no rights outside of the right to be His dependent child. I had no agendas but His, and I had no purpose outside of my calling. There were no separate compartments to my life I could call mine, nor were there any dreams apart from possessing Him and being possessed by Him. This complete consecration was necessary to ensure He became my very breath, my all in all.

My failures had taught me to **wait on** God, my challenges trained me to **wait before** Him until He moved or opened the door, my afflictions caused me to **sit** and **wait in** His presence as my ark, while coming into a place of rest in Him, knowing His timing was perfect and He was capable of working out all details without any interference from me. Standing before Him in quietness and confidence caused me to **wait with expectancy** until He gave me my marching orders to ensure I never got ahead of Him or dropped too far behind Him.[91]

It was not a matter of walking in step with the Lord; rather, it was about coming under His yoke, but I needed to invite Him to come beside me and then it was up to me to come under His yoke to keep in step with Him.

I was aware that so much of who I was, what I thought, how I walked, and how I responded had been transformed in the light of His character and love. I often felt overwhelmed by His grace, humbled by His love, sobered by His righteous ways, and at awe because of His greatness.

---

[90] Exodus 33: 12-17; Luke 2:49; 1 Corinthians 7:22,23; 2 Corinthians 5:20; 2 Timothy 2:3,4
[91] Psalm 40:1,2; 130:5,6; Isaiah 40:31; 63:9

The more I discovered about Him, the less I knew of Him. The deeper He went in me, the more aware I became of unending heights of His glory that I would never reach in this lifetime, remembering that, "Eye hath not seen, nor ear heard, neither have entered into the heart of man, the things which God hath prepared for them that love him."[92]

It became clear to me that His transforming love had changed me. It had gone deep into my character, changed and enlarged the borders of my heart, and gave me glimpses of the coming glory that reminded me once again that God's love is not only transforming, it is ongoing like flowing rivers, and eternal like the vastness of the heavens.

Come, Let Us

The excitement of the handmaidens who had heard her description of her beloved, and then heard his description of her had greatly escalated. They had been pointed to the source of love and attraction in her relationship with her beloved, but now they realized that she was the product of their love. She served as an example of its fruit, the actual visible, living testimony of it.[93]

It was clear that her beloved's love for her had transformed her and had defined the person she was and would become. It was now the handmaidens who were describing what they were seeing in her life. It was obvious from what they were declaring that his love for her had brought out the potential of her beauty, established her royalty, and prepared her to walk in her high calling according to the strength of the witness that had been developed in the inner chambers of fellowship. The Shulamite woman was clearly being brought forth as a cunning work that revealed the capabilities of the one who had been shaping her with his love.[94]

The maidens pointed to the place all life is first transmitted: the navel. They described her navel like a goblet that held an unlimited amount of wine. Wine was used as a drink offering that was poured out

---

[92] 1 Corinthians 2:9
[93] 2 Corinthians 3:3
[94] The maidens' description of the Shulamite girl begins Song of Solomon 7:1-5

by the priests, reminding her people of the blood that bound them to their covenant that identified them to life from above.[95] The fact that it was free flowing and unlimited pointed to something that is eternal.

The mention of her belly was in relationship to how real life comes from the innermost part of a person. It is like wheat that ensures life, but such wheat has always been a provision from Yahweh. The key for man to benefit and maintain life is that he must partake of the provision of God to possess it in his inner being. Granted, the first fruits of the harvest belonged to Yahweh, but such an offering ensured that He would not only receive it as a sweet savor, but once it was put on the altar and anointed with frankincense, He would bless and multiply it. Frankincense already pointed to righteousness, but once the fire was applied to this perfume, its fragrance would intensify pointing to purity emerging in new life, and when the offering was rightfully received by Yahweh, He had the freedom to bless the harvest and multiply its fruits to His people.[96]

When they mentioned her breasts, she recognized they were not in relationship to resting in love or maintaining love, but in being an extension of it to others. She knew that love can't be ministered to others unless it stands as a pillar that is balanced out by the other pillar of unfeigned faith that expresses itself in honorable actions of obedience.

Her neck was mentioned but not in relationship to armor as her beloved had pointed out in the past, but in relationship to maturity that came out of suffering.[97] She knew anything of value would first have to come to a place of maturity. It is not age that determines maturity but the willingness of the material to endure the process that will bring it to maturity, causing it to be prized by those who encounter it. Clearly, the handmaidens were seeing the great value in the love she shared with her beloved.

She had learned that to know real love it first costs you any fanciful notions about it. To overcome hindrances to real love meant ridding self of the immature ideas of it, and to grow into it meant you had to leave

---

[95] Leviticus 23:13; Numbers 15:5-7, 10; 28:7-10
[96] Exodus 23:16,19; 34:22,26,27; Leviticus 2:12-16; 23:17
[97] Song of Solomon 4:4

the old behind. Love clearly had cost what was familiar to her but not eternal. However, what really transformed her love was experiencing the type of suffering that did not come from the loss of the foolish and insignificant, but it came during the times she had disappointed her beloved.

The handmaidens' description of her eyes revealed that the love she now had was being reflected. Pools aren't deep like a well, hidden like a cistern, or free flowing like a fountain; rather, they are shallow, ever open to the light penetrating every nook and cranny, making them transparent and reflective of the terrain underneath. It was clear that the deep, hidden place of fellowship she had with her beloved had made their love pure and transparent to the onlookers.

"Heshbon" pointed to understanding a matter and what she now understood about love could only come through revelation from above. "Bathrabim" reminded her that she now was part of a larger company, a unique company that blended together as one to serve as a greater witness of that which was superior.

The mention of her nose for the first time made her realize that her love was no longer gullible or fickle. Before when it came to love, she had operated from an emotional aspect, causing many of her senses to be cast to the wind without anchor to hold them or any type of real discipline to steady them. Her experiences had taught her that her feelings were unreliable.

The concept of "nose" pointed to discernment. This was an important confirmation to her because she no longer allowed her eyes to be stirred up by surface beauty, the sensation of touches to cause reason to flee, hearing to be tainted by what she wanted to hear, and her taste buds to determine the quality of something simply by taste. She was quite aware that smell is a hard sense to seduce. If something smells bad it's probably bad, no matter how good it looks or the reputation it may carry. A bad smell will make the taste buds repel away from anything that is foul.

The way of discernment always marked the high ground of Lebanon where one is no longer subject to fleshly judgments, but is now able to discern between good and evil.[98] Damascus pointed to her ability to even discern the fragrances and their sources. For her, there was only one fragrance she wanted to smell, the heavenly fragrance of her beloved.

Carmel which means "fruitful place" or "park," pointed to the distinction that the love she shared with her beloved brought to them. Carmel was a mountain which possessed the most striking characteristic features of the country of Palestine. Its ridge served as the only headland of lower and central Palestine that formed it southern boundary. Its bold bluff almost ran into the very waves of the Mediterranean while extending southeast from a little more than twelve miles, where it suddenly terminates in a bluff, somewhat corresponding to its western end.[99]

It was clear that their love produced fruit in a beautiful garden of fellowship. It became an inner boundary to her that was highlighted by excellence that clearly transformed her attitude and had extended itself to others.

The fact they described her hair as purple pointed to the fact that she was royalty, crowned with authority. She was clearly being identified to a king and his kingdom by these handmaidens. Who would have thought that a mere Shulamite girl, such as herself, would ever be seen in such a light?

As she was thinking of what she had heard, her beloved's voice was heard once again. "How fair and pleasant art thou, O love for delights!"[100] It was clear there was expectation, excitement, and agreement in his voice and words toward what he had already heard. The word "pleasant" pointed to one being delighted, and it was clear that it was their love that was bringing a variety of delights to his heart.

When he mentioned her stature, she realized he was acknowledging that her love for him had high standing and was now erect, sure, and stable. The palm tree was in reference to her love now being deeply

---

[98] 1 Corinthians 2:10-14; Hebrews 5:12-14
[99] Smith's Bible Dictionary
[100] Song of Solomon 7:6

rooted, reaching into the fountains of the deep in order to produce fruitfulness that others could feed on and greatly benefit from.[101]

He stated his intentions, "I will go up to the palm tree, I will take hold of the boughs thereof: now also thy breasts shall be as clusters of the vine, and the smell of thy nose like apples; and the roof of thy mouth like the best wine for my beloved..."[102] This was an incredible description to her as to how he viewed their love.

Her beloved wanted to take hold of what now had become a sweet love that had been brought to maturity. Maturity is what allows one to partake of the fruit that was becoming increasingly prized by those who had tasted it in some way. It was not only sweet to the taste but to the smell. Their love had become a fragrance greatly prized by them, desired by those who witnessed it, and wished for by those who still dreamed of it. The reality of such love is rarely obtained because it can only be experienced when love has been transformed, set free from the hold and influence of the age that had initially defined it.

The description of the clusters being part of the vine revealed that the source of her love no longer originated with her. She was connected to an eternal vine because of love. Her life, inspiration, and purpose now came from the true vine of heaven, leaving her to simply be an extension of the fruit to those who partook of it.[103] The fruit would produce the best wine, a wine that would be matured in the best of environments, and as a result preferred above all others.

This precious wine was something that would demonstrate to be an acceptable offering to Yahweh, establishing a witness of a covenant that would prove to be superior to those who would but taste it in good faith. The wine would prove to be smooth to those who understood the sweetness of the union established between them, resulting in enjoyment and satisfaction. It would awaken others to speak of its delightful qualities that pointed to oneness of agreement and intimate fellowship.[104]

---

[101] Song of Solomon 7:7
[102] Song of Solomon 7:8,9a
[103] John 15:1-8
[104] Song of Solomon 7:9

Everything that was said and all that she heard brought such reveling to her spirit that she no longer could contain herself. She declared, "I am my beloved's, and his desire is toward me."[105] Although there had been similar declarations during their relationships, it was a bit different in the sense that she was declaring his desire was now her desire. There would be no separate agendas, priorities, and goals on her part. His heart was now her heart, his agenda was hers, his priorities would become what was important to her, and she would take possession of the same goals he possessed.

In the past her beloved was always the one who invited her to come away with him, but now that she understood what was important to him, she needed to invite him to come with her, and where would she take him? They would go forth together into the harvest field.[106]

She no longer belonged to one place. She had become a sojourner in the world she once knew and a pilgrim in search of the place where she would dwell with her beloved, whose very presence would identify their home. As the shepherd, her beloved would always be tending and seeking his sheep. As the king, he would take personal interest in the matters of the kingdom and the people he had been entrusted with. There was much to attend to, and she needed to confirm that she would ever be by his side in whatever field they were in. It was obvious that it was time for her to take the initiative to invite him.

They needed to go to into the fields and villages to check out the welfare of those who labored in both places to encourage and inspire. They needed to get up early to go into the vineyards to offer any needed or necessary assistance to ensure the quality of the fruit. At the gates where all business was transacted, they needed to partake of the fruits to see it they were pleasant and acceptable when it came to representing his kingdom.[107] She had clearly become a good fruit inspector, enabling her to know whether the fruit was reaching its potential. In some cases, she would take the liberty to lay up the best of

---

[105] Song of Solomon 7:10
[106] Song of Solomon 7:11
[107] Song of Solomon 7:11-13

the fruit for her beloved to share with him in the right place and at the right time in recognition of their labor together.

A Defining Moment
(The Second Companion)

The former slave girl was overwhelmed that the attention of the onlookers had turned towards her. In a way, she understood their interest, but in another way, she knew that the only thing she ultimately could do was point the inquisitive seekers back to her Lord.

She also realized from personal experience before she could direct them in the right way, she had to understand what they were seeking. To point them back to her Lord without personal interaction would seem like she was simply putting them off or placating them. It was clear that those who continued to follow her had graduated from mere observers to sincere pursuers of something that had captured their attention.

It was also becoming more obvious that she alone could have not captured their attention. She had met them in a time of personal inner chaos. They were people who lived in the shadows of the night, but now they seemed to be seeking for something they perceived she possessed.

She turned to face the encroaching group. It was obvious that not all were there that she had first encountered, but it was apparent that the ones who came to her were not as obscure as before, for they were genuinely seeking answers.

She sighed within herself as she remembered. How many times did she seek answers to only find indifference in her time as a slave? How many times did she need someone to simply notice her and care enough to smile or offer a kind gesture to add a bit of sunshine to her dreary day, or a tiny ray of hope to penetrate the darkness upon her soul? How many times did she want to stand on the highest pinnacle and cry out to the crowd to see if anyone would take note of her? She couldn't count the times she wanted to push through the crowd to touch someone who might stop and look at her and actually see a person.[108]

On that day at the auction block, her Lord had seen her and took note of her. That day she was taken off the auction block and given a new life. She realized she had come too far to not consider each of these individuals. They were people, often lost in the midst of humanity. Like her past plight, these individuals had been passed by many people who simply would look through, look past, and look around them without really seeing that they were human, an actual person who had silent dreams and were being pulled down by a vacuum of hopelessness.

That was and is the plight of humanity. Although all of humanity starts out in the same boat, all will eventually jump ship as the boat begins to sink. They flounder in the ocean of life while seeking some form of rescue to avoid drowning in the hopelessness that often grips their souls. Some become bitter as they see no rescue on the horizon, others become depressed as rescue seems to elude them, and some give up and give way to the dark shadowy waters of death, but there are those who look upward and cling to the small sliver of hope that there is a God in heaven who hears the desperate cries of one who is about to perish.

She was on that sinking boat and had found herself floundering among others who were also about to perish as a result of being swallowed by the indifference of humanity. It was in her darkest moment that she looked up and she saw him, she saw the one who saw her in her desperation and heard the secret cries of her heart, and pulled her out of her plight while lifting her above it to experience a new life.

As the seekers stopped before her, she had to ask, "Why do you seek me? After all, you followed me to my master."

The one who had asked her what was so important about her Lord that she should risk much in the night to seek him answered the question. "It's true you led us to your Lord, but we have no relationship with him. We want to know how we might enter into such a relationship so we, too, can become part of his household and perhaps even sit at his table. It's clear that he's a good master and Lord."

---

[108] Luke 8:43-48; 19:1-10

She had already noted that they didn't have a relationship with her Lord, but she thought by simply leading them to him that it would be enough. At that moment her mission was becoming defined. It was not enough to lead people to her Lord, she had to prepare them to meet him.

From past experience, she recognized their symptoms. These people felt too ashamed to even approach him. They had not realized that it was in hopelessness she had sought a deliverer, in desperation she had looked up from the auction block, and in a time of revelation she chose him as her Lord and it was in darkness that she had risked all to find him.

She smiled at them. "Follow me.[109] I was about to go to my Lord and invite him to walk with me through the villages to reach out to those in darkness, to the fields to help and encourage the workers, and through the kingdom to establish the heirs in their proper places. By following me, you will see who my Lord is and what it means to have a relationship with him that will rightfully place you in his household."

The former slave girl who now was taking her place as the bride of her Lord was now ready to take the responsibility of her position, not only to go where her Lord walked, but to take the initiative to invite him to walk beside her as she followed him into the barren, dry, dark places to secure his kingdom with him as a legacy in tribute to his greatness as king and to his fair and compassionate leadership as Lord.

She felt satisfaction in her spirit, for true rest had come to her soul. The latest search had indeed brought her to a most important defining moment of her life. She now knew her position, understood her purpose, and could see her ultimate destination.

---

[109] 1 Corinthians 11:1

Mature Love

Establishing His Likeness

Love will reflect the person you have allowed yourself to become. For the saint, godly love gives him or her the liberty to take on the likeness of Jesus. I realized that to be an effective Christian in the world meant I needed to reflect Christ, and Romans 8:29 and 2 Corinthians 3:18 confirmed that very reality. I clearly was not here to reflect my best; rather, I was here to reflect God's glory, the glory of His only begotten Son.[1]

To reflect Jesus pointed to the work of sanctification. As I learned of Jesus and set my face to follow Him in the ways of righteousness, the Holy Spirit began to do a deeper work of sanctification in me. In the hustle and bustle of daily activities, we as believers, can begin to think we are personally responsible to somehow become a mirror that reflects heavenly glory, a vessel that somehow produces the Living Water that brings life, rather than hold and maintain it, and the instrument that we must fine-tune to declare that glory to others.[2]

In sanctification you are being set apart unto God to do His work and bidding. You are becoming a refined vessel that has been made fit by the Potter to be placed among other vessels in His household to be used according to His calling upon your life.[3]

One of the simple truths I had to be reminded of was that It was God's work in and through me that counted and not what I did for Him. Philippians 1:6 says as much, "Being confident of this very thing, that he which hath begun a good work in you will perform it until the day of Jesus Christ."

The Apostle Paul made this statement, "For the which cause I also suffer these things: nevertheless I am not ashamed: for I know whom I have believed, and am persuaded that he is able to keep that which I

---

[1] John 1:14
[2] Romans 6:13; 15:16; 2 Corinthians 4:7; 2 Timothy 2:19-21; 1 Peter 1:3
[3] 2 Timothy 2: 19-21

have committed unto him against that day" (2 Timothy 1:12) The godly virtues that flowed through my life did not find their origins with me, but from God. I was simply the vessel He used to channel these virtues through in order to touch others.

The big struggle in the Christian walk is to keep to the center of what is true and important, while wading through the darkness of the present age and staying true to the glory of the next age that awaits every believer. I know I am sealed by the Holy Spirit and an heir of an eternal inheritance, but I am still in this body, ever wrestling with my humanness.[4] I dare not let down my guard until I know that I have entered into all the Lord has for me.

In the past I have complicated the simplicity of the Gospel, erected a Jesus who was hard to relate to, and an unfeeling God who was more interested in straightening me out rather than leading me to places that allowed me the freedom to reach my potential of reflecting His glory.[5]

Each failure put me back on the right path, and in my journey to discover God I became increasingly aware of His love. In God's abiding faithfulness in my life I realized the great width of God's love can never be measured.[6] God incredible love had become my initial inspiration to seek Him out and it was His abiding love during my faltering times that strengthened me to look up instead of within and around. It was the heavenly touch of His love that caused me to grow in my relationship with Him, and the faithfulness of His love that brought a greater transformation in my relationship with Him. Each encounter and revelation of His love revealed that His love is beyond description.

As the years have passed and my tabernacle is waning from age, I have noticed that my personal strength often ebbs into a whimper at the end of the day and my enthusiasm to accomplish much for His kingdom gives way to the reality that no great feat is done overnight. At this point in my life, instead of displaying patience in irritating situations, I seem to have lost all patience. I know the great test for many saints is to not allow weariness to take hold of the soul when the body is speeding towards

---

[4] Ephesians 1:11-14
[5] 2 Corinthians 3:17,18; 11:3
[6] Romans 8:38,39

its finality and the spirit is struggling to maintain its edge. We must not allow the present challenges to wear our patience down, for we are told we must possess our souls in patience so we can stand confidently in the darkness of the present age until it parts, and we have the clarity to see our Jesus in His glory.[7]

In spite of struggles of feeling far from reflecting my Lord's likeness at times, I must continue to occupy as I wait for the Lord's next move, knowing what I must focus on. I must be a vigilant watchman over my soul as I guard it against the darkness of the time in which I live. I must watch the gate of my heart to combat spiritual coldness from creeping in that causes my heart to become indifferent instead of remaining tender and willing before the Lord.[8] I must make sure there is no breach in my wall that protects the secret place of communion with Him due to weakness in my walk that may be the result of compromising with the world. I must maintain that which will establish the life of Jesus in me in a greater measure so that I can ultimately serve as a reflection of His glory in the darkness.

I must constantly remember I am a gem, who is being brought to my full potential. The Lord has not given up on me regardless of my flaws. Rough edges are being sanded off here and there while the water of the Holy Spirit polishes me during the tumbling process in order to bring out the priceless reflection of my Lord. There is nothing grand about the process, and it only makes sense that my irritations in it will not cause me to feel great about myself.

Following Jesus initially required me to carry a cross, but I know at this stage of my life I'm running a race with everything in me. This race has required me to discipline my ways, but it also has required me to leave much of the residues of my old life and this world behind. In order to leave it behind, I had to count it as being dung and the only way I could do this was by keeping in mind what I would be gaining in the end.[9]

---

[7] Daniel 7:25; Matthew 24:27; Luke 21:19
[8] Matthew 24:42-47; Luke 19:13
[9] 1 Corinthians 9:23-27; Philippians 3:7-14; Hebrews 12:1

As the times become darker, I must take the opportunity to reflect the light of Christ in greater measure. The night is obviously coming when no man will be able to work. I do not know when the light will end so that all work will cease and the darkness will enfold me into obscurity, but I must be prepared at all times. I realize that my main focus, whether in light or darkness, is to keep pressing forward to the finish line, which will mark not only the end of my personal race, but the entrance into what is eternal and glorious.[10]

In trying times I've had to take stock to keep my focus by remembering Jesus wore a crown of thorns so I could be presented with a crown of righteousness. He took the beatings for me so that I could stand before the Judge of the Universe and be declared not guilty. He allowed Himself to be placed on a cross so I could avoid tasting the death penalty. He took on my humiliation so I could be clothed in His righteousness.[11]

He became my example as He prepared my course and He became my life line as the cross identified me to His work of sanctification and redemption. I knew at the end of my life that one day I would experience greater liberty and resurrection as I exchange my cross with a crown.

The Apostle Paul talked about the crown of righteousness. I can't count the times that I have read 2 Timothy 4:7-8 to ponder and challenge myself, "I have fought a good fight, I have finished my course, I have kept the faith: Henceforth there is laid up for me a crown of righteousness, which the Lord, the righteous judge, shall give me at that day: and not to me only, but unto all them also that love his appearing."

It is a battle to finish the course and I must fight it in order to keep the faith. I do not want to assume anything about my course because when I have done so in the past, I ended up taking detours. I do not what to make presumptions about my enemies in fear that I will take them too lightly and lose my edge to discern and identify them. And, I do not want my faith to waver because my sole reliance is not on Jesus.

There are four elements in gaining the prize. It is clear that I must finish the course to receive the prize, fight the good fight if I am to

[10] John 9:4,5
[11] 1 Corinthians 1:30; 2 Corinthians 5:21

advance forward towards the destination, and walk according to the map of His Word if I am to stay the course.[12]

Finally, the fourth element is that of expectation. I must be living in expectation of His coming. The inspiring and enduring virtue behind this expectation is love. I must love His appearing. In other words, I must want to see Him because He is the heartbeat of my Christian life, the breath that enables me to walk, and the hope that will be realized.

I also know that even though I receive the crown, I will have to give it to the King of kings because He alone deserves the glory, and He alone is the only One who deserves to wear it. Like the elders in Revelation, I will no doubt cast the crown at His feet, as I bow before Him in loving adoration and worship.[13]

I'm looking for my Lord's return. I might meet Him in the air or through the door of death, but either way I'm preparing for that time.[14] Meanwhile, I occupy in faithfulness, while walking in assurance, ever persuaded that He will keep that which has been entrusted to Him against that great day of judgment.

As I watch my time wind down and darkness enfold this age, I look up knowing my redemption draws near. I do not look behind at what was, but forward as I declare the promise David declared in Psalm 17:15, "As for me, I will behold thy face in righteousness: I shall be satisfied, when I awake, with thy likeness."

And, when it comes to the present, I continue to speak in my heart what the Apostle John boldly declared in Revelation 22:20 when Jesus declared that He would surely come quickly. John's reply was simple, "Amen, Even so, come, Lord Jesus."

Taking on His Likeness

Love will become the reflection of who or what a person comes into agreement with. For the Shulamite girl her love for her beloved was allowing her to take on his likeness. She had come to a place where she

---

[12] Psalm 119:105
[13] Revelation 4:10,11
[14] 1 Corinthians 15:51-54; 2 Corinthians 5:8; 1 Thessalonians 4:13-18

walked in total agreement with him. Their relationship had gone through an incredible metamorphic state that now was taking flight in a life of service.

Her love for her beloved was clearly coming to full age but a restlessness was beginning to take hold. The more she desired to do service worthy of her beloved, the more she was met with limitations. Such limitations seemed to keep her love from fully manifesting itself in a way that would properly honor him.

She became acutely aware that it was a love that reached deep into unseen fountains that ensured its integrity and life. The refinement of the love she shared with her beloved had replaced all silliness, the deep devotion she now had towards him had pushed all fickleness aside, and she now displayed grace that spoke of her beloved's influence on her life.[15]

It was her goal to express her deep love for him, but in her culture, an outward show of affection such as a kiss, when it came to the opposite sex was only acceptable in the case of a relative such as brother. [16] Her beloved had become everything to her. She had already been established in his household as being part of the family, but the love she wanted to express was that of a bride to her betrothed.

If she could only express such love to him, she would lead him back to the city of their spiritual birth, Jerusalem where he could take her once again and embrace her close to his heart.[17] There she would eventually sit at his feet to learn more about the grace that had already shaped her attitude and service. She had long ago realized that at times she fell short of reflecting that grace to others.

Her soul desired more of her beloved so that their love could produce a greater amount of fruit that would prove to be sweeter to others.[18] She wanted others to feel the satisfaction that their love brought to her own soul, but she also realized that she needed to be filled up daily in communion with him.

---

[15] Song of Solomon 8:1,3
[16] Song of Songs, pg. 144
[17] Song of Solomon 8:2
[18] Ibid

However, she encountered various limitations that would prevent her from partaking fully of communion. Her beloved's latest absence to do the bidding of his father had taken longer than she had expected. It was true she lived in expectation of seeing him and would not let those who were around her disrupt the blessed anticipation of him coming any day.[19]

She was determined to live in such expectation due to her past failures, trusting that the next time she would see him, he would finally take her to the abode he had prepared for her. In her mind, she could see him once again coming out of the wilderness, where all disciplines are acquired by those who become wanderers in the present world and spiritual pilgrims who are diligently seeking out a place of refuge and worship.[20]

The first time he came from the wilderness, he was relaxed for his work had been done. It was clear he had come **to** her for communion, as well as **for** her so they could enjoy each other's company, but in this event, she would come with him. She would be seated with Him, leaning on him.[21] After all, she had been prepared under her beloved's careful auspice for this very occasion.

His love had allowed her room to explore, falter, grow, and fail in order to be transformed to take on his likeness as a means to reflect that which was heavenly. The Shulamite woman couldn't count the times that her beloved's love had allowed her to reach great heights to discover that the heavens could not contain his love and the darkness would never be able to consume it. It was alive, powerful, and eternal. It could never be brought down from the heights of its excellence, nor would it be rendered useless or perverted by those who wanted to use it for self-glamorization. It was protecting of one's well-being and nurturing of one's soul.

His love had kept her during uncertainty, sustained her through testing, and brought her through defeats to a place of glorious transformation that allowed her to see beyond the present world. And,

---

[19] Song of Solomon 8:4
[20] Song of Solomon 8:5; 1 Peter 2:11
[21] Song of Solomon 3:5

what she saw was great majesty that reminded her that there was so much more to discover about her beloved's love, so much more to experience because grace was its channel, goodness its point of integrity, and truth its immovable foundation.

She also was aware that this expectation had to be occasionally stirred and as a result had asked her beloved to set a seal upon her heart that would stir up her love. It was the heart where love was seated, and her arm represented love's strength to endure. She knew that in separation genuine love could be raised up with excessive passion, and when challenged it could become jealous, causing it to become exceedingly hot once again, setting aflame her whole heart.[22]

Eternal love that has once again been rekindled into a flaming fire in a heart cannot be quenched by any testing. Whether it be the watery trials of tribulation, the deep canyons of despair, the ovens of persecution, the desolation of famine, the unveiling of unabated shame, the consuming forces of peril, and the sharpness of the sword, genuine love would prove to be the conqueror in the end.[23]

It was her desire to see her beloved come, but she was aware that there were others like her that needed to know the satisfying love of her beloved. She had long ago realized that she shared the communion of their love with nobody and that she alone held her specific place in his kingdom. Such knowledge had brought satisfying peace upon her, as well as confidence, but his heart was so big that he was capable of establishing others in a like love while making it personal and separate from his relationship with her.

She had found favor with him and he had left her behind to point tender hearts and souls to him. She had clearly been made distinct by his redemption and was capable of pointing the seeking heart to the one who stood above all other tall cedars. She also knew she was to bring necessary balance to their lives with the different pillars of graces she had acquired along the way. As she had already pointed out to others, there was no one like her beloved.[24] She had become a witness to

---

[22] Song of Solomon 8:6; Ephesians 1:13
[23] Song of Solomon 8:7; Romans 8:37-39
[24] Song of Solomon 8:8-10

others as to where they could find the entrance into a relationship with the lover of her soul so they too could obtain peace of heart, mind, and soul.

However, she was quite aware that she had been set apart for her beloved. She was the one who needed to shine, and that meant taking on his likeness and becoming a mirror to others as to the love, life, and fellowship he offered.

She acknowledged that Solomon had a vineyard at Baal-hamon. "Baal-hamon" means "the Lord of a multitude." It was clear that he had the means to lease this vineyard to others to tend to. Granted, the renter would pay him so much for the land, but they would reap the abundance of crops for themselves.[25]

Even though Solomon had an impressive vineyard, the vineyard she worked in was special. She worked in it because of her love for her beloved. The love she had was satisfying to her soul and far more attractive than the fruits of all of Solomon's vineyard.[26]

The Shulamite woman was aware that her beloved had established many gardens besides her garden, but she wanted others to be sure that when her beloved came to inspect and commune in the gardens with them that they would hear his voice and quickly respond to his invitation.[27]

The Shulamite woman had learned to hear his voice in the many arenas of the world, but the concept of a garden pointed to the fact that it was all about personal communion. One must learn how to listen for his voice before one can hear what he is saying. She so wanted to be sure of hearing his voice when he did come for the final time and call her to himself.[28]

She looked at her garden and considered all that had transpired. Now her restless soul had one simple, but heartfelt, request as she looked to the hills and remembered how quickly he had come to her in the past, bringing fragrances of life, joy, and contentment, "Make haste,

---

[25] Song of Solomon 8:11
[26] Song of Solomon 8:12
[27] Song of Solomon 8:13
[28] Ibid

my beloved, and be thou like to a roe or to a young hart[29] upon the mountains of spices."[30]

Reflecting His Likeness

Love reflects the maturity of a relationship. For the bride to be, she was now reflecting a maturity in her relationship with her Lord that had first seemed impossible to her. Looking back, she could see that she had come a long way in her attitude towards him. She no longer harbored skepticism towards his love for her, but she also knew because of her flawed attitude she could not take credit for the maturity of their love that now graced her life with various disciplines.

Their love was now defining her in every way. She was no longer reflecting the darkness of her soul and the corruption of the world, but she was now reflecting his very likeness. His influence on her had clearly cleansed her, changed her attitude, established her heart, and lined her walk up to his example and way.

Since her service began in the communities and fields of the world, she could not count the many times she had relived and retold her story to anyone who would listen. Her testimony was ingrafted in her heart and mind. She was ever reminded that she came from small beginnings and it was during her many failures in her relationship with her Lord, that he had established the forgiveness of love and its blessing of unmerited grace towards her. Each time her Lord had reconciled with her, a greater sobriety took root, reminding her to not forget that she had been purged from her old life.[31] She had been found in slavery, lost and hopeless but called by her Lord who took her hand and led her away from the darkness that had ripped at her soul. She was cleansed at his table of communion and instruction, prepared in testing, and tempered in the harvest fields of service.

---

[29] According to Smith's Dictionary, a roe is an antelope and a hart is a male stag. Both animals are swift but the hart points to a deer that has hit his prime.
[30] Song of Solomon 8:14
[31] Zechariah 4:10; 2 Peter 1:9

She kept remembering that through it all she was being made ready for his next visitation. His love for her had clearly established her on a sturdy foundation. She no longer feared the storms because she was anchored upon a rock that reached incredible depths. It was as her Lord's love reached into the depths of her soul that her spirit had been set free to reach heights that gave her glimpses into a glorious future with him.

As she held on to the promise of such a wondrous future, she realized that much time had passed since he had physically come her way. She had occasionally pondered that even though she was spiritually renewed within, time and the world were taking their toll on her. She was not getting any younger and she had to wonder at times if she could keep up her pace serving as his living witness before others, while keeping her spiritual edge of discernment. She didn't want to become weary in well doing or drop the ball when she needed to fight some fight, or fail to keep advancing on the path set before her. [32]

Daily she was soiled by the world and challenged by the endless demands that had no eternal value to them. Granted, there were times she figured out how to redeem the time by using mundane periods to pray, meditate on truth, and occasionally establish a special altar to commemorate a particular blessing and event.[33]

As the days passed by, she had to remember that her hope was not behind her but in front of her. Meanwhile, she would pray that she would be found worthy to take her place beside her Lord when he did return.[34] In the past she had been found wanting, and she knew by what he said, that his next visitation would be abrupt and only those who were ready for his return would be taken into his abode to consummate their union with him.

It was obvious that she had to keep oil in her lamp so that when he came, she could light it and make her expectation known to him.[35] She couldn't afford to be slack in the area of preparation because as with his

---

[32] Galatians 6:9,10; Ephesians 4:23
[33] Ephesians 5:15-20
[34] Luke 21:36
[35] Matthew 25:1-13

past visitations, he could easily come when least expected, especially by those who did not live in such anticipation.

She hated to admit that at times she was anxious about being ready, but she refocused on what was established in her life and on her relationship with her Lord. She had kept her heart single towards him, while avoiding the traps of the world. She had not veered off of course, and when she found herself tempted to do so, she remembered his love for her. It was his love that so often made her more than a conqueror in her walk.[36]

Even though her outer person was showing some wear and tear, she knew that one day she would put off the old and be clothed with a new body. In one way she could hardly wait, but in another way, she was aware that there was still a great work that needed to be done before he came.[37]

She remembered that her Lord warned her that he would not come back until the work was done on both ends. He was preparing a special place and she was trying to prepare those who were called to not only be ready for his visitation, but to be prepared to embrace a new life and a glorious inheritance.[38]

As she felt overwhelmed by the mission before her, she took consolation that she was not alone in carrying the burden for those in the great harvest fields of the world. Her Lord had given her assistants that enabled her to carry out her responsibility.

As she was preparing for the next day, she suddenly heard a voice that caused her spirit to leap. Had she not been waiting to hear that precious voice? And now it was calling to her, followed by the sound of a great trumpet. She suddenly felt her corruptible body falling to the way side as the incorruption of heaven took hold of her. She found herself lifted up in an instant, and she remembered the precious words of the Apostle Paul concerning the unveiling of a mystery, that in a moment, in the twinkling of an eye, the corruptible, which is attached to this present life, must put on the incorruption of her Lord's likeness, and the mortal

---

[36] Romans 8:37
[37] John 5:25-29
[38] John 14:1-3

aspect of her earthly body, must put on the immortality of a glorified body, for death was being swallowed up in complete victory.[39]

She had been sealed for that moment to realize the fullness of the glorious redemption secured by her Lord, and now nothing of the world could hold her from being part of a great wedding supper, as well as entering into all that he had promised her.[40] Incredible glory enfolded her, joy overwhelmed her soul as praise flowed from her lips, declaring the very words of the apostle in 1 John 3:2, "Beloved, now are we the sons of God, and it doth not yet appear what we shall be: but we know that, when he shall appear, we shall be like him; for we shall see him as he is."

---

[39] 1 Corinthians 15:51-56
[40] Revelation 19:5-10

The

Epilogue

The Unveiling

Remember where this story started. It began with a wrestling match within myself whether I could write this book and do it justice. I have filled the pages before you with words, but do they properly paint the picture of the lives and struggles of my two companions? It is easy to write from personal experiences, but to insert oneself into the experiences of others to present a valid picture, presents a completely different challenge.

Even though I'm at the end of this book, the challenge to show how the picture of our three lives intertwine is overwhelming. To me, connecting the dots to unveil the identity of my second companion is of the utmost importance. It is the unveiling of my second companion that is going to bring greater understanding to the reader of my personal journey, as well as the life of the Shulamite girl.

Let me begin by reminding the reader that the old Testament is full of shadows, patterns, types, and examples.[1] These shadows point to one person, the Lord Jesus Christ. The patterns point to His work of redemption, and His examples give us insight into the ways of His righteousness.

When it comes to the Song of Solomon, the shadows and patterns are prevalent. For example, the king who also came to the Shulamite girl as a shepherd to lead her into greater places of fellowship points to Jesus Christ who came into this world as a humble king in a manger in order to lead His sheep as a Shepherd into a greater life of communion and service.[2]

Like the king in the story in Song of Solomon 3:6, Jesus came out of the barren wilderness of humanity (the root of Jesse) to redeem and claim a bride for Himself. Like the king who was relaxing on the bed in Song of Solomon 3, Jesus' work ceased after redemption and He sat

[1] 1 Corinthians 10:1-6; Hebrews 8:5
[2] Matthew 2:1-6; Luke 2:4-7; John 10:1-29

194

down on the right hand of glory. Like Solomon who was waiting in the wings to be king, Jesus waited in eternity to come as king in order to not only lead His people as a Shepherd, but become the Lamb of God. Solomon was a man of peace, while Jesus, the Prince of Peace, who brought reconciliation between God and man.[3]

We must not forget the shadow of the Shepherd's hand at the door. Remember the response of the Shulamite girl after she saw his hand? She was moved in her innermost being by it. We know that Jesus will be recognized because of His nailed pierced hands. It was the prophet Zachariah that recorded, "And I will pour upon the house of David, and upon the inhabitants of Jerusalem, the spirit of grace and of supplications: and they shall look upon me whom they have pierced, and they shall mourn for him, as one mourneth for his only son, and shall be in bitterness for him, as one that is in bitterness for his first born" (Zechariah 12:10). This mourning will occur throughout the land.[4]

We also have the table of communion evident in all three stories. The Lord's greatest desire is to commune with each of us and He even stands at the door and knocks to receive entrance. We sit at the table where His Words and life is imparted to us by His Spirit, but we must learn how to assimilate them before we can know the will of God.

With this in mind, who or what shadow does the Shulamite girl cast? It is important to understand the shadow because it is what will also identify my second companion. Perhaps you already have your suspicions as to who she is, but before she is unveiled it is also vital to point out that every believer is part of her story, and without her story, I would not have my own to share. The drum roll please: The Shulamite girl is a type or shadow of the *church*. This means my third companion represents the church, the bride of Christ as presented in the New Testament.

The concept of "church" is not a new one even when it came to the Old Testament. It means an "assembly called out." The great martyr, Stephen, referred to the Israelites as the church in the wilderness in Acts 7:38. We know as Christians that we are a called-out assembly. The

---

[3] Isaiah 9:6; 11:1-5; John 1:29; Ephesians 2:13-16; Philippians 2:6-8; Hebrews 8:1
[4] Song of Solomon 5:4; Zechariah 12:11-14

Apostle Paul explained how marriage contained a great mystery which was unveiled in Christ and the church in Ephesians 5:22-33. He clarified how the church is the body of Christ in Ephesians 4:11-16 and referred to it as a building, a holy temple in Ephesians 2:20-22. Peter referred to believers as lively stones that were part of a spiritual house, and identified them as a chosen generation, a royal priesthood, a holy nation and a peculiar people in 1 Peter 2:5 and 9.

Every believer is part of Jesus' body, the church, in which He is the head. This body has been called by the Lord, cleansed and set apart by the washing of His Spirit and His Word, and anointed for service. Every Christian has been fitted into His Body as well as His household. As the body of Jesus, we do His bidding; as servants in His household we carry out the business of our Lord in the harvest fields of the world, and as God's temple we house His Spirit. We are to stand distinct in this world, ever prepared to worship Him in Spirit and truth and to represent and reflect His glory to the world around us.[5]

As eluded to, the Shulamite girl is not the first shadow of the church cast in the Old Testament. Some are hidden like the boards (many membered church) fitted in silver brackets (redemption) that formed the inner structure of the tabernacle that was covered with the coverings that pointed to the complete work of redemption, while other shadows that were found in the Song of Solomon were brought forth in living color.[6] For example, we can see beautiful shadows cast in Genesis 24. Here we have Abraham (representing the Father) sending out his servant (symbolic of the work of the Holy Spirit) to secure a bride (Rebekah) for his son Isaac (Jesus). These priceless shadows bring dimension to the ongoing revelation of Jesus in the New Testament.

Think about this for a moment. Located practically in the middle of the Bible is a poetic book that serves as the shadow, example, and type of Jesus and His church. To me, this states the importance that this revelation has to the heart of God. Clearly, we can summarize that the church existed from the beginning, not only in the heart of God, but in

---

[5] John 4:22-24; 17:17; 1 Corinthians 3:16,17; 6:19,20; 12:12-14; Ephesians 1:22, 23; 5:23, 26; Titus 3:5; Hebrews 3:1-6; 1 Peter 1:22-25; 1 John 2:27
[6] Exodus 27:8-15

His mind, and to see redemption completed, He brought it forth through His Son, and His plan was executed on an old rugged cross.[7]

The book of Solomon sets forth an important script as a prelude to the struggles of Jesus' body the church in the midst of diverse cultures and the prevalent philosophies that are forever trying to take captive each generation.[8] The Shulamite girl's journey was, and continues to be, my journey, and in all honesty, will prove to be every Christian's journey when it comes to growing into a healthy relationship with the Lord. The girl in the Song of Solomon clearly manifested the reality and challenges of the church. It is for this reason the three of us have similar experiences and growing pains.

The love story of the three of us is an example of a carnal love being captured in an unexpected way by the love of God, only to discover that it will quickly falter if not properly challenged to take root and grow spiritually into the truths and promises of God. Although it may grow, it must ultimately be transformed in preparation of the believer to not only be a recipient of the enduring, lasting, eternal love of God, but an avenue for it to flow though to others.

Like all new believers, the Shulamite girl begins with great concern because of her black condition when she first encountered the king. Due to sin, we all stand on the auction block of the world as our souls are being auctioned off to a the highest bidder, but like Rahab we can choose to believe in Yahweh and take hold of the red cord of redemption, and like Ruth we can choose to follow our Naomi to the one true God of Israel and become part of a spiritual, lasting legacy, and like the Shulamite girl we can choose to accept the King's invitation, regardless of how black our soul is and how soiled we are because of the world, to follow Him to His banqueting table where we can begin to taste of His sweet, abiding, eternal love.[9]

As you can see, the final chapter found both the Shulamite girl and me waiting for the return of our beloved King, Shepherd, and Lord, while our third companion experienced it. For the Shulamite girl she was

---

[7] John 1:18; Ephesians 1:4; Hebrews 9:26
[8] Colossians 2:8
[9] Joshua 2:18; 6:22-25; Ruth 1:14-19

seeing it in her spirit in Song of Solomon 8, as well as longing in her soul for the return of her beloved; and for me, I am looking for His return with great expectancy, but for the third companion, the church, she will see His visible return. His return is not just the church's blessed hope but her future promise to enter into His unhindered glory. The church will see her Lord descend, the clouds will part and the trumpet will sound and those who are dead in Christ will rise first to be caught up with those who remain to meet the Lord in the air, and so shall we ever be with Him.[10] What a glorious promise and future given to every member of Jesus' Body! As part of His Body, His Bride, each of us as believers will finally sit with Him at the marriage supper of the Lamb in Revelation 19:7-9. Meanwhile, each of us must live in expectancy as we continue to look up, as well as into the distant future for that time when all glorious promises will be fulfilled, and where we will bathe and rejoice in His unhindered glory forever.

Meanwhile, the church is the bride, waiting for the return of her bridegroom. May the Spirit of God be strong, enabling her light to shine in the great darkness as the incredible invitation in Revelation becomes louder, stronger, and bolder in that darkness, "And the Spirit and the bride say, Come. And let him that is athirst come. And whosoever will, let him take the water of life freely" (Revelation 22:17).

[10] 1 Thessalonians 4:16-18

Bibliography

Song of Songs, Watchman Nee, © 1965 by Christian Literature Crusade

A Dwelling Place for God, Ruth Specter Lascelle, © 1990 by Hyman Israel Specter

Strong's Exhaustive Concordances of the Bible, James Strong, S.T.D., LL.D.; World Bible Publishers

Smith's Bible Dictionary, William Smith, L.L.D. © by Thomas Nelson, Inc.

Psalms, A Devotional Commentary, Herbert Lockyer, Sr., © 1992 by Kregel Publications,

Other books by Rayola Kelley:

Hidden Manna
Battle for the Soul
Stories of the Heart
The Great Debate

Volume One: Establishing Our Life in Christ
My Words are Spirit and Life
The Anatomy of Sin
The Principles of the Abundant Life
The Place of Covenant
Unmasking the Cult Mentality

Volume Two: Putting on the Life of Christ
He Actually Thought it Not Robbery
Revelation of the Cross
In Search of Real Faith
Think on These Things
Follow the Pattern

Volume Three: Developing a Godly Environment
Godly Discipline
Prayer and Worship
Don't Touch That Dial
Face of Thankfulness
ABC's of Christianity

Volume Four: Issues of the Heart
Hidden Manna (Revised)
Bring Down the Sacred Cows
The Manual for the Single Christian Life
Parents are People Too

Volume Five: Challenging the Christian Life
The Issues of Life
Presentation of the Gospel
For the Purpose of Edification
Whatever Happened to the Church?
Women's Place in the Kingdom of God

Volume Six: Developing Our Christian Life
The Many Faces of Christianity
Possessing Our Souls
Experiencing the Christian Life
The Power of Our Testimonies
The Victorious Journey

Volume Seven: Discovering True Ministry
From Prisons and Dots to Christianity
So You Want to be in Ministry

Series:
The Christian Life Series
The Leadership Series

Devotions:
Devotions of the Heart: Book One and Two
Daily Food for the Soul: OT and NT

Gentle Shepherd Ministries Devotion Series:
Being a Child of God
Disciplining the Strength of our Youth
Coming to Full Age

Nugget Books:
Nuggets From Heaven
More Nuggets From Heaven
Heavenly Gems
More Heavenly Gems